TODAY'S SPECIAL

This book is dedicated to Frédérique, Max and Otis,
for making my life complete.

All recipes serve 6-8
unless otherwise stated

introduction

MY WIFE IS A PARISIENNE BUT HAS FAMILY IN THE AUVERGNE AND PROVENCE. SO WE TRAVEL EXTENSIVELY IN FRANCE, ALWAYS TAKING THE LONG ROUTE SOUTH, WITH BIKES ON BOARD, MAKING NUMEROUS STOPS EN ROUTE TO SAMPLE LOCAL SPECIALTIES. OUR EXPERIENCES ON THESE JOURNEYS LARGELY INSPIRED MY COOKING AND THE DIRECTION IN WHICH I WANTED OUR RESTAURANTS TO GO.

My early career, working with some of the UK's finest chefs, brought me to the conclusion that simplicity, generosity and hospitality are the crucial elements that make a restaurant great. In 2005, after the sale of Putney Bridge, my business partner Will Smith, my wife and young son Max and I took some time out travelling to New York and France, to figure out what people look for in a restaurant, whether top-end or small family-run. We were unanimous in wanting an informal approach, value for money and no-frills satisfying seasonal food – the philosophy of Arbutus was forming.

In terms of concept and ethos, Arbutus is no more than a bistro moderne, part of a movement that has flourished in Paris, but has had only a slow steady rise in London. To us such restaurants have more soul, passion and common ground with the general public.

Of course, a modern bistro concept, built around the *plat du jour* or 'today's special' and a glass of wine, means that seasonality is crucial, as is searching for the lesser known produce and resurrecting forgotten cuts of meat, such as pig's head, belly of veal and ox tongue. Most restaurants ignore these in favour of better-known cuts – but they have to pay a premium for them and they miss out on the flavour of the tougher cuts. The sourcing of ingredients for quality and cost can be time-consuming, but it is an exercise that has to be done daily.

Our wine philosophy

Another aspect of the bistro we wanted to adopt was that glass of wine to accompany the *plat du jour*. Will and I had always wanted diners to have a greater choice of wines by the glass. We had decided that our wine list was to be just 25 bins each of reds and whites, plus a few sweet wines and champagnes, so we boldly decided to offer everything in carafes of one-third of a bottle.

The staff would be trained in the different styles of wine on the list and what to recommend with what dish. The wine list itself would become user-friendly, set out on a single piece of paper and priced from cheap to expensive, so you could quickly find your price point. No heavy leather-bound booklet, no sommelier to sniff at your choices… and none of those worrying moments trying to find something you can afford.

Value was always an overriding factor, so it followed that one-third of a bottle carafes must be one-third of the price of a bottle. This encourages people to try wines more appropriate to their meal rather than some catch-all for the table. It also allows the more adventurous to try a top-end wine without having to fork out £100 on a bottle. Most of all, we wanted our customers to feel confident about their choices, knowing we would replace anything they didn't like, even if there was nothing actually wrong with the wine.

CHILLED CUCUMBER
SOUP WITH SMOKED
SALMON ❖ CHILLED PLUM
TOMATO GAZPACHO,
ANDALUSIAN STYLE ❖
ROAST TOMATO SOUP
WITH MASCARPONE ❖
MUTTON BROTH ❖ SOUPE
AU PISTOU ❖ CHESTNUT
AND SWEET ONION SOUP
WITH TROMPETTE
MUSHROOMS ❖ ROAST
PUMPKIN SOUP ❖ CORNISH
RED MULLET WITH
GREEN OLIVE TAPENADE ❖

Chilled cucumber soup with smoked salmon

The subtle flavour of the cucumbers used is obviously what this soup is all about, so this is definitely a case for avoiding the Dutch hothouse types and going for a good organic supplier. Don't be tempted to avoid the salting and degorging process: cucumber juices may be less bitter than they once were, but they are still fairly indigestible.

SERVES 4

5 cucumbers

15g salt

2 tablespoons full-fat crème fraîche

300ml full-fat milk

FOR THE GARNISH

4 teaspoons crème fraîche

4 slices of smoked salmon

Pinch of smoked paprika

Young shoots, such as shiso, coriander shoots or mizuna

Peel the cucumbers, halve them lengthwise and deseed 4 of them. Slice these into a bowl and add the salt to degorge them for about 10 minutes. Rinse well and drain.

Place the degorged cucumbers in a blender with the crème fraîche and milk, and liquidize until very smooth. Strain through a fine-meshed sieve and chill for at least 3 hours or until very cold.

To serve, dice the remaining cucumber. Pour the soup into 4 soup plates and arrange the crème fraîche, salmon slices and diced cucumber over the top, then sprinkle with smoked paprika and young shoots.

Chilled plum tomato gazpacho, Andalusian style

This soup is so easy to make. I peel the peppers for the garnish with a potato peeler to make them more digestible, or you can even roast them and peel them, or use more piquillo peppers. Piquillo peppers are small tangy peppers from Navarra in northern Spain. They are roasted in open fires, then peeled by hand and packed in their own tasty juices.

1.5kg plum tomatoes

400g tin or bottle of piquillo peppers

1 cucumber

1 celery stalk

4 tablespoons red wine vinegar

4 tablespoons Worcestershire sauce

200ml good-quality extra-virgin olive oil

2 slices of bread

Few splashes of Tabasco sauce

Salt

FOR THE CROUTONS
2 thick slices of white bread

Olive oil for drizzling

FOR THE GARNISH
1 red pepper, deseeded and diced

1 yellow pepper, deseeded and diced

¼ cucumber, peeled and diced

1 small red onion, diced

1 small bunch of mint, leaves torn

1 small bunch of basil, leaves torn

Olive oil

Blend the tomatoes, piquillo peppers with their juices, cucumber, celery, vinegar, Worcestershire sauce, oil and bread, together with Tabasco and salt to taste, until smooth and creamy. Pass through a fine sieve until it is the consistency of double cream. If you like, you can repeat the sieving several times for a very refined soup. Adjust the seasoning with more vinegar, Tabasco, Worcestershire sauce and salt if necessary (remembering that chilling mutes the flavours of such seasonings). Chill.

Make the croutons by toasting the slices of bread, then drizzling them with olive oil afterwards and cutting them into 5mm cubes.

When the soup is well chilled, serve scattered with the garnishes and croutons.

Roast tomato soup with mascarpone

We were travelling with some friends in Italy, trying to find a place to stay in the Chianti region. Even though it was very late in the afternoon, the little country inn we eventually found offered us lunch as we obviously looked tired and hungry. This wonderful soup was rustled up in minutes and served with delicious chilled local *vino bianco* and chunks of their own bread.

SERVES 4-6

1.5kg plum tomatoes

Sea salt

About 100ml extra-virgin olive oil, plus more for serving

1 large onion, finely chopped

3 garlic cloves, thinly sliced

1 teaspoon chilli flakes

1 teaspoon fennel seeds

8 good-quality anchovy fillets

Sprig of rosemary, chopped

8–12 spoonfuls of mascarpone cheese

Preheat the oven to 200°C/gas 6.

Halve the tomatoes, arrange them cut side up in a roasting pan in a single layer and sprinkle with salt. Roast for 10–15 minutes until soft and darkened in colour. Allow to cool, then chop coarsely, including the skins.

In a heavy-based pan, heat the olive oil and gently cook the onion, garlic, chilli flakes, fennel seeds and anchovy fillets until the onion is translucent and the anchovies have dissolved.

Add the chopped tomatoes with all their juices, the rosemary and a splash of water if a bit dry. Bring to the boil, then take off the heat. The soup should be chunky.

Dot the mascarpone over the soup and drizzle with olive oil to serve.

Mutton broth

This is definitely one of those soups that benefit from being made the day before. Cooking the lamb on the bone will add even more flavour to the soup and, when I make it at home, I don't even bother to take the meat off the bone to serve.

200ml olive oil

300g diced mixed vegetables (ideally carrots, onions, leeks, turnip and celery)

4 garlic cloves, crushed

300g neck of lamb on the bone

30g pearl barley, rinsed

Bouquet garni

Salt and freshly ground black pepper

Good handful of chopped parsley

Ideally the day before, heat the olive oil in a large heavy-based saucepan and lightly sweat the vegetables and garlic in it.

Add the lamb, barley, bouquet garni and 2 litres of cold water, and bring to the boil. Skim, taking care not to remove any vegetables. Season with salt and pepper. Continue simmering until the lamb is cooked through, about 2 hours. Adjust the seasoning, if necessary.

If you like, you can serve this as it is, but if you prefer to serve it with the lamb off the bone, leave it to cool slightly. When cool enough to handle, lift out the lamb and flake the meat from the bones. Add this back to the soup and reheat.

Either way, finish with a scattering of chopped parsley.

Soupe au pistou

On my first visit to Provence, a friend's grandmother introduced me to this lovely fresh soup, full of the flavours of the surrounding countryside. As with anything so supremely simple, the freshness of the ingredients is all-important – as is the quality of the oil used. Pistou is a popular Provençal condiment much the same as Genovese pesto.

SERVES 4–6

200g onions

200g carrots

100g leeks

200g squash or pumpkin

250ml good-quality extra-virgin olive oil

200g potatoes

200g courgettes

Bouquet garni

Salt and freshly ground black pepper

100g fresh peas or broad beans, blanched

100g cooked fresh white beans (Coco de Paimpol, see page 41, or other)

4 tomatoes, skinned, deseeded and chopped

100g cooked short-cut macaroni or ditali

FOR THE PISTOU

3 garlic cloves

1 bunch of basil

50g freshly grated Parmesan cheese, plus more for serving

About 100ml good-quality extra-virgin olive oil, plus more for serving

Peel the vegetables as necessary, and cut them into rough 1cm dice. Rinse the leeks well.

In a large heavy-based pan, sweat the onions, carrots, leeks and squash or pumpkin in the olive oil over a gentle heat until soft. Add the potatoes and courgettes, and sweat these gently, stirring, until just beginning to soften.

Just cover with water, add the bouquet garni, with salt and pepper to taste, and cover with a lid. Bring to the boil, lower the heat and simmer until all the vegetables are tender. Add the remaining ingredients and set aside to keep warm.

To make the pistou, combine all the ingredients except the oil (in a food processor rather than a blender, as this gives a better consistency). Then, with the machine still running, pour in just enough oil to make a thick, smooth paste.

Remove the bouquet garni from the soup and add the pistou at the last minute, together with a drizzle of olive oil and more grated Parmesan.

Chestnut and sweet onion soup with trompette mushrooms

You can make this delicious autumnal soup with any type of wild mushroom or even ordinary chestnut mushrooms. For a touch of luxury, sprinkle over a little shaved truffle as you serve it.

75g butter

2 white onions, finely chopped

4 garlic cloves, thinly sliced

1 teaspoon chopped thyme

1 teaspoon chopped rosemary

200g fresh or frozen chestnuts, thinly sliced

100g trompettes des morts mushrooms, well cleaned and picked over

100g chestnut mushrooms, thinly sliced

200ml Madeira

1.5 litres chicken or vegetable stock or water

Salt and freshly ground black pepper

1 teaspoon chopped tarragon

1 tablespoon chopped parsley

Melt the butter in a large heavy-based pan, and cook the onions, garlic, thyme and rosemary in it until the onions are translucent, about 5–10 minutes.

Add the chestnuts and cook lightly for a further 5 minutes. Stir in both types of mushroom and cook for a further 2 minutes. Pour in the Madeira and reduce by two-thirds. Add the stock or water, bring to the boil and simmer for 15 minutes.

Finish with salt and pepper to taste, and scatter over the chopped tarragon and chopped parsley.

Roast pumpkin soup

The flavour of the soup is so much more intense if the pumpkin is roasted beforehand. I always try to use the variety Ironbark when available, as it has a very good strong colour and sweet flavour.

1 small pumpkin

Splash of olive oil

100g butter

1 onion, finely chopped

2 garlic cloves, chopped

Sprig of rosemary, chopped

Sprig of sage, chopped

½ teaspoon freshly grated nutmeg

1 tablespoon honey

Salt and freshly ground black pepper

Fresh goats' curd, very fresh goats' cheese, fresh ewes'-milk ricotta or mascarpone, to serve

Preheat the oven to 160°C/gas 3. Cut the pumpkin into equal-sized segments and remove the seeds. Wrap in foil and roast in the oven until soft, about 45–60 minutes. Set aside to cool.

Heat the olive oil and butter in a large heavy-based pan and cook the onion until just softened. Add the garlic, rosemary, sage and nutmeg, and continue cooking for a couple of minutes.

Spoon the cooked pumpkin flesh over the onion mixture, discarding the skin, and combine well. Use an old-fashioned potato masher to crush the pumpkin. Add enough cold water to give the soup a thick broth-like consistency and bring to the boil. Add the honey, salt and pepper, and simmer for 20 minutes. Adjust the seasoning, if necessary.

Dot with the fresh goats' curd or cheese to serve.

Cornish red mullet soup with green olive tapenade

Other than bouillabaisse this is one the most luxurious fish soups you can make. You could also make it with gurnard, or a mixture of red mullet and gurnard. We make the tapenade with the big meaty Spanish green olives called Gordal Reina, from the quality Spanish food importers Brindisa, which have a wonderfully subtle and unique flavour.

1kg whole red mullet, preferably Cornish

3 tablespoons olive oil

1 small onion, chopped

1 small carrot, chopped

1 small fennel bulb, chopped

7 large over-ripe tomatoes, halved

8 garlic cloves, crushed

Sprig of rosemary

300ml white wine

100ml Ricard or Pernod

1 tablespoon tomato paste

Salt and freshly ground black pepper

Squeeze of lemon juice

Squeeze of orange juice

Slices of fresh country bread, to serve

FOR THE GREEN OLIVE TAPENADE

Large handful of stoned green olives (see above)

Small tin of anchovies in oil, drained

1 tablespoon salted capers, rinsed

Splash of olive oil

First make the tapenade: put all the ingredients in a blender and process until smooth.

Cut the whole red mullet into three lengths. Don't worry about removing the head and guts, as these are integral to the flavour of the soup.

Heat the oil in a heavy-based pan and fry the pieces of fish until golden in colour, then take out and reserve. Add chopped vegetables, including the tomatoes, together with the garlic and rosemary, to the pan and sweat until soft, but do not allow them to colour much.

Add the mullet back to the pan with the alcohol, bring to the boil and boil rapidly for 2–3 minutes. Add the tomato paste and cover with cold water. Bring to the boil again, skim and simmer for 18–20 minutes.

Pass the soup through a mouli sieve, extracting all the juices. You could blend in a liquidizer, but I find the result not as good.

Now pass the soup through a very fine sieve. Return to the heat, bring to the boil and skim. Lower the heat and reduce to a good soup consistency.

Finish with salt and pepper to taste, and a squeeze each of lemon juice and orange juice.

Serve with the tapenade spread on slices of fresh country bread.

Fish

WARM CARPACCIO OF ORGANIC
SCOTTISH SALMON WITH SPICED
SHALLOT VINAIGRETTE ❧ SALAD
OF SLOW-COOKED SALMON
WITH SWEET-AND-SOUR YOUNG
ONIONS ❧ CORNISH GURNARD
WITH WARM À LA GRECQUE
VEGETABLES ❧ COD WITH
SPINACH BEET, TOMATO AND
CORNISH WINKLES ❧ ROAST
PLAICE WITH FENNEL ❧ BAKED
WHOLE WILD SEA BREAM WITH
FRESH WHITE COCO BEANS ❧
TARTARE OF MACKEREL WITH
PICKLED CUCUMBER ❧ CORNISH
POLLOCK, POTATO GNOCCHI,
WARM TOMATO AND ANCHOVY
VINAIGRETTE ❧ HALIBUT WITH
ROAST BABY GEM LETTUCE ❧
SMOKED EEL, CHELTENHAM
BEETROOT AND HORSERADISH ❧
SQUID AND MACKEREL BURGER
WITH SEA PURSLANE AND
PARSLEY JUICE ❧

Warm carpaccio of organic Scottish salmon with spiced shallot vinaigrette

It is essential when giving salmon this treatment that you first get the grill really good and hot, and that you only flash the fish under it very briefly – just long enough for it to start turning opaque. Do not allow it to cook all the way through or it will become dry. The Merlot/Cabernet Sauvignon vinegar really imparts just the right balance of sweet and sour flavours. If you can't get them, any very good-quality red wine vinegar or even a fine balsamic will be almost as good.

500g thinly sliced organic Scottish salmon

Maldon sea salt

Handful of young shoots, ideally coriander, or chives

FOR THE SPICED SHALLOT VINAIGRETTE

6 large shallots, finely chopped

20g butter

100ml extra-virgin olive oil, plus more for drizzling

Sprig of thyme, chopped

Pinch of crushed chilli

2 tablespoons runny honey

100ml Merlot vinegar or Cabernet Sauvignon vinegar

200ml full-bodied red wine

First make the spiced shallot vinaigrette: lightly sweat the shallots in the butter and oil with the thyme and chilli until the shallots are translucent. Add the honey and bring to the boil. Add the vinegar and reduce by two-thirds. Add the red wine and reduce until syrupy. Set aside.

Preheat a hot grill.

Arrange the salmon on serving plates and dot the vinaigrette all over it. Drizzle with a little olive oil, sprinkle over a little Maldon sea salt and quickly flash under the hot grill until the salmon just goes opaque.

Finally strew some young shoots or chives over the top to serve.

Salad of slow-cooked salmon with sweet-and-sour young onions

Micro cress salad or micro greens are grown like mustard and cress and harvested when the seeds have sprouted and formed their first leaves. The tender seedlings have intense flavours. We get them from Secretts Farm in Surrey, where they call them 'baby leaves'. They grow a range that includes wild rocket, Italian red dandelion, red amaranth, golden mustard, ruby chard, red mustard, sorrel, red orach, tatsoi, golden purslane, fine cress and mizuna. They even sell pots of growing mixed leaves by mail order.

1 fillet of salmon, about 1kg, skinned and any pin bones removed

4 ripe tomatoes, sliced

1 lemon, sliced

1 garlic clove, thinly sliced

sprig of thyme

1 tablespoon chopped parsley

100ml olive oil

Splash of white wine or vermouth

Salt and freshly ground black pepper

4 young Sweet Gem lettuces, separated into leaves

Micro cress salad, to serve

Good crusty bread, to serve

FOR THE SWEET-AND-SOUR YOUNG ONIONS

50g butter

300g young onions or shallots, peeled but root left attached

2 tablespoons caster sugar

100ml good-quality white wine vinegar (we use Forum Chardonnay vinegar)

Preheat the oven to 150°C/gas 2.

First prepare the sweet-and-sour young onions: in a heavy-based pan, melt the butter, add the onions and cook them gently until golden all over. Add the sugar and gently caramelize it. Pour in the vinegar (it will spit and seethe, but don't worry) and stir gently with a wooden spoon. Reduce until syrupy. Now just cover with cold water and simmer until syrupy once again. Check to see if the onions are soft to the touch; if so, leave to cool in the glaze, otherwise cook a little longer.

In the base of a roasting pan big enough to hold the salmon, first put the tomato slices, lemon, garlic, thyme and parsley. Drizzle with half the olive oil, a splash of wine and 50ml water, then season with salt and pepper. Bring to the boil, place the salmon fillet on top, season that and cover with foil.

Bake in the preheated oven until cooked medium rare, about 20 minutes. Leave to rest, still covered, until cool. During this period the juices will all mingle together.

Gently lift the salmon out and keep warm. Reheat the roasting pan gently, add a splash of water if it has become dry and strain the liquid through a fine sieve, gently forcing all the juices through.

Gently toss the lettuce leaves lightly in olive oil and season. Arrange on serving plates, flake the salmon over, add the glazed onions and pour over the juices. Top with some micro cress salad and serve with some good crusty bread.

Cornish gurnard with warm à la grecque vegetables

Gurnard is a rather undervalued fish, possibly because it is a bit bony and, being a bottom feeder, it can have a slightly earthy taste. It does, however, have a lovely sweet flavour. This recipe would also suit grey or red mullet, and even mackerel or other oily fish. The vegetables also make a good lunch or supper dish on their own.

6 medium fillets of gurnard

FOR THE À LA GRECQUE VEGETABLES

8 tomatoes, blanched, skinned, cut into quarters and deseeded, reserving all the trimmings

150ml olive oil

½ teaspoon coarsely ground black pepper

½ teaspoon coarsely ground coriander seeds

3 shallots, sliced into rings

Maldon sea salt

2 medium carrots or 6 small young carrots, peeled or scraped and sliced

2 garlic cloves, thinly sliced

1 bay leaf

1 small cauliflower, cut into small florets

1 small head of fennel, thinly sliced

Handful of chanterelle (girolle) mushrooms, rinsed and dried

Grated zest and juice of 1 large lemon

Handful of picked flat-leaf parsley

1 teaspoon freshly picked marjoram or summer savory

Ask the fishmonger to scale, fillet and remove any pin bones from the gurnard.

Prepare the vegetables: put 400ml water in a pan and add all the tomato trimmings. Bring to the boil and simmer for 10 minutes. Strain the stock, pushing all the tomato juice through. Set aside.

Heat 100ml olive oil gently in a large saucepan. Add the pepper, ground coriander seeds, sliced shallots and ½ teaspoon Maldon salt. Cook for about 3 minutes. Add the carrots and reserved tomato stock. Bring to the boil with the garlic and bay leaf, and simmer for about 10 minutes. Add the cauliflower and simmer for about another 5 minutes, then add the fennel and mushrooms and cook for another 5 minutes. By now all vegetables should be almost cooked but still retain a little crunch.

Add the lemon zest and juice, the parsley, marjoram and tomato pieces, with more salt if needed. Bring back to the boil, then leave to cool. This is just a vinaigrette flavoured by all the vegetables being cooked in the stock and acidulated by the lemon and herbs at the final stage.

Cook the gurnard in the remaining olive oil in a large frying pan over moderate heat until slightly firm, about 5 minutes, seasoned with Maldon sea salt and freshly ground black pepper. (You may have to use two pans or cook in batches.)

Serve the fish with the vegetables. This dish can be eaten cold, but is so much nicer served warm.

Cod with spinach beet, tomato and Cornish winkles

For the ethically minded, cod has been off the shopping list for some time, but there are now several sources of sustainable cod, be it from colder more northerly waters, like Icelandic cod, or line-caught cod – there is now even highly acclaimed farmed cod from the Shetlands. So do check that your cod comes from a sustainable source.

SERVES 4

100g winkles

100g butter

4 pieces of cod, each about 160g

100ml olive oil

1 garlic clove, crushed

Sea salt and freshly ground black pepper

Grated zest and juice of 1 lemon

200g spinach beet, stalks separated from the leaves

2 shallots, finely chopped

6 plum tomatoes, quartered and diced

1 tablespoon chopped parsley

Wash the winkles in plenty of cold water, then leave to soak in fresh cold water with a tablespoon of salt for about 20 minutes. I find this helps to degorge any sand or grit that they hold.

Drain, cover again with cold water and bring to the boil, then simmer for about 20 minutes or until they can be easily pulled from the shell. Pull away from the shell and discard the little door or lid (the operculum). Reserve the meat.

Heat a non-stick pan, add 80g butter and wait until it foams. Add the pieces of cod, together with a splash of olive oil, the garlic and salt and pepper to taste. Cook the fish gently, basting frequently. It should take on a nut-brown colour. Finally add the juice of ½ the lemon and baste well. Take off the heat and leave to cool in the pan. Set aside on a separate plate and keep warm.

In the same pan, add the stalks from the spinach beet, season and cook until almost soft. Then add the leaves and finish cooking for a few minutes until these wilt. They will take on all the brown butter and juices from the fish. Set aside and keep warm.

In the same pan, put the remaining butter and olive oil, and fry the shallots for 2 minutes, without allowing them to colour. Toss in the tomatoes and the winkles, together with the lemon zest and parsley. Add a little seasoning and more lemon juice to taste. Serve with the fish and spinach beet.

Roast plaice with fennel

Illustrated on previous page

This is a very seasonal fish. From September to November large plaice are abundant and relatively cheap. Their flesh is very dense and steak-like. Don't buy the little immature plaice available at other times of the year, both for reasons of sustainability and flavour.

SERVES 4

1 large whole plaice, skin on

Knob of butter

Splash of olive oil

Sea salt and freshly ground black pepper

3 fennel bulbs, outer layer discarded and bulbs split

1 garlic clove, crushed

Sprig of lemon thyme

Sprig of rosemary

Sprig of marjoram

4 tablespoons miniature capers or chopped larger capers

Splash of Ricard

Ask the fishmonger to split the plaice down the backbone and portion into 4 pieces each roughly 200g.

Preheat the oven to about 150°C/gas 2.

Heat a non-stick ovenproof pan large enough to take the 4 pieces of fish and add a knob of butter and a splash of olive oil. Pat the fish dry and season with salt and pepper. When the butter has melted and started to sputter, add the fish, white skin down (the dark skin will peel off when cooked, while the white skin has a better, gelatinous flavour). To crisp the white side, keep the heat pretty high. When it is golden in colour, flip the pieces over and repeat on the dark side, basting as you do so.

When cooked, transfer to the preheated low oven to finish cooking through – this shouldn't take more than 5–7 minutes. Remove from the oven but leave it on. Keep the fish covered in a warm place.

Drain and reserve all the fat and juices. Wipe the pan with some paper towel, place it back on the heat and add a splash of olive oil. When hot, add the pieces of fennel and colour these all over. Add the garlic, shredded herbs, capers, Ricard and some seasoning, together with the reserved juices and fat from the fish, and bake in the oven until the fennel is slightly soft but still with a bit of crunch, about 10 minutes.

Serve with the plaice and the juices poured over.

Baked whole wild sea bream with fresh white Coco beans

The Coco de Paimpol is a white bean grown in the Côtes d'Armor region of Brittany. The term Paimpol comes from the port of the same name, where it is believed the beans were first imported from South America in the 1920s. They are now a staple of the Breton diet and their harvest between July and October is eagerly awaited. It was the first vegetable in France to be awarded *Appellation d'origine contrôlée* status.

SERVES 4

1 whole large sea bream, scaled, gutted and fins cut off

Olive oil

FOR THE BEANS

500g fresh white beans, such as Coco de Paimpol, or good-quality dried

1 small onion

1 celery stalk

1 carrot

2 garlic cloves, finely chopped

1 bouquet garni

Sea salt and freshly ground black pepper

50g chopped flat-leaf parsley

Well ahead, prepare the beans: shell them if fresh, place in a saucepan with the onion, celery, carrot, garlic and bouquet garni. Add enough water to cover the beans by 5cm. Bring to the boil – do not add salt at this stage or the exteriors of the beans will harden – and simmer gently until cooked, about 40 minutes.

When nearly tender, season the beans and strain through a colander, reserving 200ml of the cooking liquid and discarding the vegetables and bouquet garni. Put the beans on a tray to cool down.

Preheat the oven to 160°C/gas 3. Put the fish on a baking tray, liberally coat with olive oil and season generously. Bake in the preheated oven for about 20 minutes or until the thickest part of the fish (the back) gives under pressure. Take out and leave to rest a little.

To serve, reheat the beans in the reserved stock, add the parsley and a splash of olive oil, and adjust the seasoning if necessary.

Peel the skin off the fish, season and serve with the beans.

Tartare of mackerel with pickled cucumber

This tartare treatment would suit several other types of oily fish, particularly meaty tuna, but you could also use sardines or salmon.

8 mackerel fillets, skinned

2 tablespoons capers, rinsed, drained and finely chopped

2 shallots, finely chopped

4 tablespoons finely chopped parsley

1 teaspoon finely chopped fresh ginger

Grated zest and juice of ½ lemon

Grated zest and juice of ½ lime

200ml double cream

Baby coriander shoots, to garnish (optional)

Smoked paprika, to garnish (optional)

FOR THE PICKLED CUCUMBER

½ cucumber peeled, halved lengthwise, deseeded and thinly sliced

Salt and freshly ground black pepper

2 tablespoons runny honey

2 tablespoons white wine vinegar

First salt the cucumber slices well and leave to drain in a colander.

Prepare the mackerel: remove the central bones from the fillets (the bones should come out in one piece if this is done carefully). Chop the flesh into small dice, about 5mm.

In a bowl, mix this with the chopped capers, shallots, parsley, ginger, lemon and lime juices, salt and pepper. Chill in the fridge.

Make the pickled cucumber by bringing to the boil all the pickle ingredients apart from the cucumber in a pan with 4 tablespoons of water. Take off the heat and add the cucumber. Leave to cool.

Lightly whip the double cream to ribbon stage (the whisk leaves a trail in the cream), add the citrus zest with a squeeze of the juice of each and some seasoning.

Using two wetted serving spoons, mould the cream into quenelles and place one on each serving plate, heap some mackerel tartare alongside that and finish with some of the cooled pickled cucumber.

If you like, garnish with some coriander shoots and sprinkle the cream with smoked paprika.

Cornish pollock, potato gnocchi, warm tomato and anchovy vinaigrette

Pollock is again much underrated, probably because, even more than most fish, it has a very short shelf-life and needs to be super-fresh for you to enjoy its mild, sweet flavour. Its flesh can also have a rather grey colour, which doesn't appeal on the slab.

SERVES 4

4 shallots, finely chopped

150ml olive oil, plus more for drizzling

8 anchovy fillets, drained and rinsed

12 ripe best-quality tomatoes, blanched, skinned and roughly chopped

4 garlic cloves, crushed

1 teaspoon fennel seeds

½ teaspoon ground coriander seeds

1 teaspoon dried herbes de Provence

2 pinches of crushed chilli flakes

Salt and freshly ground black pepper

1 tablespoon miniature capers

4 handfuls of cooked gnocchi (see page 144)

4 pieces of pollock, each about 200g

Young basil shoots, to serve (optional)

In a heavy-based pan, sweat the shallots in the olive oil until soft, then add the anchovies and continue cooking until these dissolve. Increase the heat and throw in the tomatoes, which will soften quickly over a high heat. Add the garlic, fennel and coriander seeds, the dried herbs and the chilli flakes. Cover and simmer for 30–40 minutes, stirring occasionally.

After this time, check the consistency of the sauce: it should be like that of thick vinaigrette, but not too soupy. Adjust the seasoning if necessary, add the capers and gnocchi, and place the pollock fillets on top. Cover again and heat for another 10 minutes. This should cook the fish and heat the gnocchi through.

To serve, carefully lift the fish out and place on a warm plate. Spoon the vinaigrette into shallow soup plates, flake the pollock and scatter it over, then drizzle with olive oil and serve. Some young basil shoots would go well with this.

Halibut with roast Baby Gem lettuce

Although Atlantic halibut are over-fished, abundant Pacific halibut are available from Alaska. Cooking the Baby Gems in this way, rather like the Italians do with radicchio, brings out the innate sweetness that makes them perfect to serve with fish.

SERVES 4

100g butter, plus an extra knob for the lettuces

3 tablespoons olive oil, plus more for the lettuces

Sea salt and freshly ground black pepper

4 halibut steaks on the bone, each about 200g

4 whole Baby Gem lettuces, halved lengthwise

Splash of Noilly Prat or dry vermouth

Sprig of rosemary, chopped

About 6 sprigs of lemon thyme

2 garlic cloves, finely chopped

2 tablespoons double cream

Squeeze of lemon juice

Preheat the oven to 150°C/gas 2.

In a large non-stick frying pan, heat the butter and olive oil until hot. Season the fish with salt and lightly colour the steaks on both side in the pan, basting as you go. Lower the heat and continue cooking, still gently basting. When cooked, leave to rest in the pan and keep warm.

In another non-stick pan, melt the knob of butter with a slug of olive oil over a highish heat and colour the lettuce halves on their flat cut sides. Add a splash of Noilly Prat, the herbs, garlic and seasoning, and bake in the preheated oven until tender, 10–15 minutes.

Now lift the fish and lettuce halves on to serving plates. Add the fish cooking liquor to the lettuce cooking liquor, mix in the double cream and boil to reduce it to a good sauce consistency. Adjust the seasoning, add a squeeze of lemon juice, spoon over the fish and serve.

Smoked eel, Cheltenham beetroot and horseradish

Make sure you source a good-quality smoked eel. We buy ours from the Dutch Eel Company in Lincolnshire, which rather surprisingly is the only eel merchant based in the UK. Serving the eel warm with the remaining ingredients at room temperature makes the whole ensemble much more appetising.

Cheltenham beetroot, more correctly Cheltenham Green Top Beetroot, is one of the oldest varieties of this underrated native vegetable. It is long in shape, very sweet and has a fine earthy flavour. A good greengrocer will be able to source if for you and many good farm shops and pick-your-owns have it.

1 large fillet of smoked eel, about 400g

8 cooked Cheltenham beetroots

Young watercress or land cress sprigs, to garnish (optional)

FOR THE BEETROOT PURÉE

150g cooked Cheltenham beetroots

1 teaspoon runny honey

Salt and freshly ground black pepper

Splash of olive oil

Squeeze of lemon juice

FOR THE HORSERADISH CREAM

200ml double cream

2 tablespoons horseradish relish

First make the horseradish cream by whipping the double cream to soft peaks then folding in the horseradish to taste. Chill.

Make the beetroot purée by blending all the ingredients together with a little water, if necessary, to make it spoonable but keeping a shape.

Cut the eel into individual portions, about 65g. Just before you want to serve, you need to take off the skin. This is made much easier by warming the fillet: put it under a low grill in the bottom of the grill pan and turn it from time to time.

Serve the pieces of eel with the beetroots, beetroot purée and the horseradish cream. Garnish with sprigs of young watercress or land cress, if you like.

Squid and mackerel burger with sea purslane and parsley juice

When we first opened Arbutus, we had on the menu brochettes of squid and mackerel – a favourite combination of mine – but they didn't prove very popular. I thought I would try using the ingredients to make a sort of pâté instead and, by some accident, ended up making these burgers, which are now among our most popular items.

Chopping the squid and mackerel with a knife can be a tedious task, but the results are so much better than if you use a mincer or food processor. We serve these burgers with a juice of parsley and sea purslane to give them a sea-fresh finish, but you can just serve them with a parsley juice and any favourite salad leaves.

MAKES 4

150g razor clams

2 good splashes of olive oil

1 glass of white wine

200g cleaned squid (frozen to tenderize it)

4 medium-to-large mackerel fillets, all bones removed

1 tablespoon chopped coriander

1 tablespoon grated ginger

1 tablespoon chopped garlic

1 teaspoon lime zest

Sea purslane and/or your favourite salad leaves

FOR THE PARSLEY JUICE

1 bunch of flat-leaf parsley

Large handful of sea purslane (optional)

Salt and freshly ground black pepper

First prepare the clams: all razor clams are sandy and need soaking and washing in plenty of cold water. Drain well.

Heat half the olive oil in a large pan with a tight-fitting lid and add the clams (they will sizzle but don't worry). Add the wine and cover quickly. Shake the pan to disturb them, still covered, and cook for about 3 minutes. Take off the heat and drain over a colander, reserving the cooking juices. When cool, pull the meat from the shell and reserve.

To prepare the parsley juice, briefly blanch the picked parsley and purslane, if using it, in a litre of boiling salted water. Drain, reserving some of the liquid, and then refresh in cold water. Drain again and liquidize with a couple of tablespoons of the reserved blanching water and a little of the clam cooking juice to give the consistency of a vinaigrette. Season if necessary and set aside.

Chop the squid and mackerel finely using a chef's knife. In a large bowl, mix these with all the remaining ingredients except the oil, purslane and cooked clams. Leave to chill in the fridge for a couple of hours.

When well chilled, preheat the oven to 200°C/gas 6 and mould the mixture into 4 thick (about 2cm) burgers (you can use cling film to hold the shape). Remove the cling film if using and fry in the olive oil over a high heat until a good golden colour, turning once. Transfer to the oven for 3 minutes only to let them cook through. Do not overcook either in the pan or in the oven, so they stay moist.

Serve garnished with the cooked razor clam meat, parsley juice and purslane or salad of choice.

poultry & game

POT ROAST PHEASANT WITH
BACON * WOOD PIGEON WITH
SPÄTZLE, CHESTNUTS AND
POMEGRANATE * WILD DUCK WITH
ROOT VEGETABLE PURÉE,
WALNUTS, CELERY AND GRAPES
* RABBIT À LA MOUTARDE WITH
ROAST SWEET ONIONS * ROAST
SADDLE OF RABBIT WITH
SHOULDER AND LEG COTTAGE PIE *
JUGGED HARE WITH SOFT POLENTA
AND PARMESAN * ROAST VENISON
WITH SWISS CHARD * LEMON AND
GARLIC ROAST CHICKEN WITH
SWEET-AND-SOUR CARROTS *
GLAZED CHICKEN WING PIECES
WITH CRUDITÉS OF SPRING
VEGETABLES * FRICASSÉE OF
CHICKEN LEGS WITH LYONNAISE
POTATOES * ROAST COQUELET,
SPATCHCOCK-STYLE WITH A SAUCE
OF TENDER YOUNG GARLIC *
CHICKEN OYSTERS SOT-Y-LAISSE
WITH PEAS AND MACARONI *

Pot roast pheasant with bacon

These days, pheasants are intensively farmed and fattened up before the corporate shoots, leading to lacklustre and flavourless birds. They seem to have lost their lean gamy characteristics over the years. If you do get the chance, however, buy a brace of hens with pliable breastbones (a normal sign of age, as the stiffer the breastbone the older the bird). The result will be well worth it.

SERVES 4

Knob of butter

2 hen pheasants

Splash of neutral-flavoured oil, such as groundnut

8 slices of streaky bacon

4 juniper berries, crushed

2 sprigs of sage

2 garlic cloves, crushed

Sprig of thyme

100ml sweet cider

Preheat the oven to 170°C/gas 3½.

In a heavy-based pan big enough to hold the 2 birds (and which has a lid), colour the birds all over in the butter and oil. Remove and reserve.

Throw the bacon into the pan, followed by the rest of the ingredients except the cider and lightly colour. Add the cider and bring to the boil.

Add the pheasants on their sides, cover with the lid and cook in the preheated oven for 8 minutes. Take out and turn the birds over on to the other side, then cover and cook for a further 8 minutes (the covering both speeds up the cooking and also keeps the birds moist). Check to see if they're cooked: a gentle squeeze of the breast at the thickest point (towards the winglets) should indicate this. Baste with all the juices until ready to serve.

Serve the birds with the bacon and some of the pan juices.

Wood pigeon with spätzle, chestnuts and pomegranate

Spätzle or spaetzle, meaning 'little sparrows', consists of tiny noodles or dumplings, and is a common accompaniment in Germany and Alsace, especially for dishes with lots of gravy. The basic dough can be rolled and cut like pasta or gnocchi, but is more commonly forced through a colander as here. There are purpose-made devices that work like potato ricers, but this method gives results that are just as good.

SERVES 4

4 wood pigeons, wishbones removed

Good splash of olive oil

110g butter

2 garlic cloves, crushed

Sprig of thyme

2 shallots, finely chopped

2 medium carrots, peeled, diced and cooked

60g cooked chestnuts

Seeds from 1 pomegranate

1 tablespoon chopped parsley

FOR THE SPÄTZLE

30g warm melted butter

2 whole eggs plus 1 extra egg yolk

250g plain flour, sifted

120ml full-fat milk

Salt and freshly ground black pepper

Freshly grated nutmeg

First make the spätzle: in a large mixing bowl, mix the butter with the eggs, then add the sifted flour. Pour in the milk gradually and beat well for about 5 minutes. Finish with salt, pepper and 2 gratings of nutmeg (this is all ideally done in a mixer with the paddle attachment). The consistency will be like that of a loose dough. Leave to rest for 30 minutes. Preheat the oven to 190°C/gas 5.

Bring a pan of salted water to a simmer. Add small amounts of the spätzle mix to a wide-holed colander and, using a plastic scraper, force the mix through into the simmering water. You are aiming for small dumpling/gnocchi-type pieces. Cook for 1 minute, drain and set aside.

In a heavy-based ovenproof pan, brown the wood pigeons in the oil and 50g butter. Season well, add the garlic and thyme, and roast in the preheated oven for about 7 minutes. Ideally, leave them pink and juicy. Remove from the oven and leave to rest in the pan.

Melt half the remaining butter in a heavy frying pan, add the spätzle and lightly colour over a high heat. Season, then take out and set aside. Add the rest of the butter and the shallots to the pan and cook until the shallots are softened. Add the carrots and chestnuts, then return the spätzle to the pan and warm everything through. Finally add the pomegranate seeds, parsley and a spoonful of juice from the pigeon pan. Adjust the seasoning.

To serve, carve the pigeons in half, leaving the legs attached. Spoon the remaining pan juices over each bird and add the spätzle, carrot, chestnut and pomegranate mixture.

Wild duck with root vegetable purée, walnuts, celery and grapes

You can use any type of wild duck – mallard, widgeon or teal, although as teal are smaller you would need two per person. I normally use mallard and I find that because of their diet the skin can have a quite fishy taste, so I remove it before serving.

SERVES 4

4 whole wild ducks

Vegetable oil

1 garlic clove

1 bay leaf

Sprig of thyme

10 black peppercorns

1 large glass of brandy or Armagnac

1 large glass of port or full-bodied red wine

1 teaspoon redcurrant jelly or honey

FOR THE ROOT VEGETABLE PURÉE

2 carrots, peeled and cut into small pieces, trimmings reserved

1 small swede, peeled and cut into small pieces, trimmings reserved

3 garlic cloves

80g butter

FOR THE WALNUTS, CELERY AND GRAPES

1 small bunch of celery

Splash of olive or vegetable oil

2 handfuls of fresh wet walnuts, shelled and peeled

½ bunch of black Muscat grapes

Ask your butcher to remove the legs and rear part of the back from the ducks, reserving the breasts on the crown for roasting. Get him to leave the legs intact but chop the back into smallish pieces for the stock/sauce needed to start this recipe.

Colour the legs and chopped pieces of back in the vegetable oil in a heavy-based pan. Add the garlic, bay, thyme, vegetable trimmings and peppercorns, and continue to colour until all are nicely browned. Add the brandy, bring to the boil, then add the port or red wine and bring back to the boil. Add the redcurrant jelly, cover with water and bring to the boil yet again. Adjust the seasoning, if necessary. Skim and simmer until the leg meat can easily be pulled from the bone, about 1 hour.

Take the legs out, pull the meat away from the bones and reserve, discarding the bones. Strain the remaining stock/sauce, forcing as much through as possible. Reserve. Preheat the oven to 180°C/gas 4.

To make the root vegetable purée, put the carrot and swede pieces in a pan, add the garlic, a knob of butter and a little salt, then barely cover with water. Bring to the boil and simmer until tender. Liquidize in a food processor until smooth. Adjust the seasoning, if necessary.

To prepare the celery: cut away the stems so that you have just the stalks. Peel off the tough strings and discard. Cut the stalks into 7.5cm lengths and lightly colour in another knob of the butter. Add 200ml of your duck sauce plus 100ml water, season and cook until the celery is tender. Drain, reserving the juice, then add it to the rest of your duck sauce. Warm the walnuts and grapes in the sauce.

To a large pan or roasting tray, add a splash of olive or vegetable oil and lightly colour the ducks all over in it. Place in the preheated oven for about 10 minutes. The ducks do not take long to cook and should ideally be served pink, or the meat will be tough and dry.

Remove from the oven and let rest for about 8 minutes. Take off the breasts and remove the skin if you wish (see above). Carve the breast meat and serve with the root vegetable purée, celery and the sauce with the walnuts and grapes.

Rabbit à la moutarde with roast sweet onions

This is basically a classic French bistro dish, normally '*aux deux moutardes*' – that is, made with two different types of mustard. I actually prefer it with just the Dijon.

Salt and freshly ground black pepper

6 rabbit legs

100g butter

100ml white wine vinegar

3 tablespoons Dijon mustard

500ml chicken stock or water

150ml double cream

1 tablespoon dried oregano

1 teaspoon smoked paprika

1 teaspoon chopped rosemary

6 garlic cloves, crushed

2 bay leaves

Roast Sweet English Onions (page 158), to serve

Season the rabbit legs. Melt the butter in a heavy-based casserole and colour the rabbit all over in it. Take out of the casserole and reserve.

Swill the casserole with the vinegar and boil to reduce by two-thirds. Add all the remaining ingredients and bring to the boil. When boiling, add the rabbit back to the casserole, cover and cook gently until the meat falls freely from the bone.

Take out the rabbit and set aside. Boil the cooking liquor to reduce it to a sauce-like consistency (it will coat the back of a spoon). Adjust the seasoning and return the rabbit to the pot to warm through.

Serve the rabbit with the juices and the roast onions.

Roast saddle of rabbit with shoulder and leg cottage pie

Get your butcher to prepare the rabbit by removing the front and back legs, taking off the head and splitting it in half, and cutting out and reserving the liver(s) and kidneys, then removing the ribcage and backbone from the saddle without piercing the skin. The two loins of meat should remain intact.

1 large tame rabbit (or 2 fat wild rabbits), including the liver and kidneys

Salt and freshly ground black pepper

2 large pieces of pigs' caul

2 knobs of butter

2 splashes of olive oil

1 large carrot, diced

1 celery stalk, diced

1 onion, diced

4 garlic cloves, peeled and split in half

100ml white wine vinegar

300ml white wine

1.25 litres chicken stock

6 tomatoes, blanched, skinned and chopped

1 bay leaf

Sprig of rosemary

1 tablespoon chopped tarragon

1 tablespoon chopped parsley

Potato Purée (see page 131), to serve

Season all the bits of rabbit with salt and pepper. Put the offal down the centre between the loins of meat, then roll the saddle, encasing the offal, and wrap the roll in the caul and tie in place. Leave to chill in the fridge.

To make the cottage pie: melt a knob of butter with a splash of olive oil in a heavy-based pan and colour all the remaining rabbit pieces, including the head and backbone, until golden. Lift out and set aside. Now add another knob of butter and splash of olive oil, and colour the vegetables and garlic. When they are coloured, return the browned rabbit to the pan, add the vinegar and reduce it almost completely away. Add the wine and reduce that by two-thirds. Add the chicken stock, tomatoes, bay and rosemary, bring to the boil and skim. Simmer gently for about 2 hours, until the meat is tender.

Preheat the oven to 170°C/gas 3½. Lift the rabbit out and set aside, then reduce the stock to a good sauce-like consistency. Strain the sauce, reserving the vegetables (you will need these for the pie). Pull the meat from the bones and combine with the vegetables and chopped herbs. Taste and adjust the seasoning. Put the mixture into a pie dish with a few tablespoons of the sauce (the remaining sauce will be for the finished dish) and a drizzle of olive oil. Top this with potato purée.

Put the cottage pie to bake for 40 minutes before you intend to roast the saddle.

Take the saddle(s) from the fridge about 30 minutes before roasting to come to room temperature (meat should never be roasted straight from the fridge, as the exterior will become overcooked and tough). Season with salt and pepper, colour lightly in a pan and roast in the preheated oven alongside the pie for about 10–15 minutes.

Leave to rest for 8 minutes, then carve and serve alongside the cottage pie.

Jugged hare with soft polenta and Parmesan

The best polenta for this is Bramata, which we use in the restaurants and can be found in all good Italian delis. Just follow the packet instructions, but use half milk and half water for the liquid and cook for at least an hour (the longer you cook it the more the flavour develops), then add freshly grated Parmesan and good olive oil to taste.

4 legs and 4 shoulders of hare (plus 3 tablespoons of hare's blood if available)

Flour, for dusting

Salt and freshly ground black pepper

2 knobs of butter, 1 chilled

Vegetable oil for frying

500ml full-bodied red wine

1 litre light chicken stock or water

FOR THE MARINADE

2 garlic cloves, crushed

Sprig of thyme

1 bay leaf

8 juniper berries, crushed

300ml pineapple juice

FOR THE POLENTA

300g polenta (see above)

About 750ml milk

250g freshly grated Parmesan cheese, plus more for serving

about 100ml good olive oil

The day before, make the marinade by mixing all the ingredients in a large bowl. Toss the pieces of hare in the marinade to coat well and leave to marinate in the fridge overnight.

Next day, remove the hare from the marinade and pat dry. Strain the marinade and reserve. Season the flour and lightly coat the hare in it. Melt a knob of butter with a splash of oil in a heavy-based casserole and sear the floured hare until lightly coloured all over. Add the reserved marinade, red wine and stock or water. Bring to the boil, skim and simmer gently until cooked – the meat should be almost falling off the bone, about 1½–2 hours. The shoulders may be cooked before the legs; if so, carefully lift them out and reserve while the legs finish cooking.

While the hare is cooking make the polenta as described above, mix in the grated Parmesan and olive oil, and season to taste.

When all the hare is cooked, take the pieces out of the liquid and keep warm. Bring the liquid to a simmer and add the blood, if you have it, together with a knob of chilled butter, and adjust the seasoning. Finally, add the reserved meat back to the liquid. If you have used the blood, do not allow the liquid to boil again after adding or this will give the sauce a grainy texture.

Serve the hare with the sauce and the polenta, sprinkled with more grated Parmesan.

Roast venison with Swiss chard

We find that the haunch of venison has a better flavour than the saddle and it is also significantly cheaper. Get the butcher to section the haunch into good-sized portions, removing all sinew. The pineapple juice may seem odd but I like to marinate my game in this as it contains the enzyme bromelain, which helps tenderize the meat. It also gives it a little sweetness and most game benefits from that. Redcurrant jelly is also a classic addition.

Swiss chard is a fantastic and versatile vegetable, often ignored and still not readily available. There are numerous varieties, but we tend to use only the green variety, which has a creamy and slightly bitter taste. It is so much better for being cooked or braised for a long period, thus partners all roast meat perfectly and makes an excellent gratin. I wouldn't use it with fish, however, as its flavour could be too dominant. When buying Swiss chard, choose the younger tender stems, as they require less work. The older ones are coarser and the stems need to be peeled like celery.

6 portions of venison haunch, each about 200g

60g butter

Salt and freshly ground black pepper

FOR THE MARINADE

4 juniper berries, crushed

2 slivers of orange zest

2 tablespoons pineapple juice

200ml olive oil

2 garlic cloves, crushed

Sprig of rosemary

FOR THE SWISS CHARD

6 large stems of Swiss chard

Splash of olive oil

2 garlic cloves, crushed

A few hours ahead, prepare the marinade by mixing all the ingredients in a large bowl and put the meat to marinate in it in the fridge for about 3 hours before cooking.

About 15 minutes before you want to serve, prepare the Swiss chard: wash it well, cut the stems into desirable lengths and tear up the leaves. Sauté the stems in the olive oil with the crushed garlic, salt and pepper until tender. Add a splash of water, then add the leaves, cover and cook slowly until both stems and leaves are tender, about 8–10 minutes.

Heat the butter in a heavy-based pan until it is hot enough to sear the outside of the steaks. Take the meat from the marinade, reserving that. Pat the meat dry and season with salt and pepper, then cook for about 5 minutes on each side until medium rare. Leave to rest for another 5 minutes on a warm plate.

Add the juices from the rested meat to the pan with 2 spoonfuls of the marinade, adjust the seasoning and spoon over the meat. This dish doesn't need a sauce, just the juices and marinade.

Serve the venison with the cooking juices and the chard.

Lemon and garlic roast chicken with sweet-and-sour carrots

Illustrated on previous pages

The removal of the wishbone from a bird prior to trussing helps it cook more evenly, makes it much easier to carve when it is cooked and also means that you gain a bit more meat. Savory is used a great deal in Provençal cooking and is a favourite herb of mine. Like a cross between thyme and mint, it can be quite assertive, especially the winter variety, which is very citrusy and should be used with care.

1 best-quality chicken, about 2kg

1 lemon, halved

1 head of garlic, split across in half

Sprig of summer savory

1 clove

Salt and freshly ground black pepper

Large knob of butter

Splash of olive oil

FOR THE SWEET-AND-SOUR CARROTS

500g carrots, preferably young, peeled and cut into pieces if large

50g butter

50g sugar

100ml white wine vinegar

Sprig of thyme

Sprig of rosemary

1 garlic clove, crushed

Preheat the oven to 180°C/gas 4.

If you like, prepare the chicken for roasting by removing the wishbone and trussing the bird.

Stuff the chicken with the lemon halves, garlic, savory, clove and seasoning. Also season all the outside.

Heat the butter and oil in a roasting pan. Add the chicken sideways on one leg and cook in the preheated oven for 18 minutes. Turn over on to the other leg and cook for another 18 minutes. Baste now and again, but not too often. Finally turn the chicken on its back and finish roasting for another 15 minutes.

At this point, prepare the Sweet-and-sour carrots: lightly colour the carrots in the butter, then add the sugar and cook, tossing, to caramelize them for about 3–5 minutes. Add the vinegar and reduce by two-thirds. Just cover with water (about 500ml), then add the thyme, rosemary, garlic, salt and pepper. Bring to the boil and simmer until the carrots are just tender, about 15–20 minutes. Lift the carrots out and set aside. Boil the cooking liquor to reduce it by two-thirds, place the carrots back in the liquid and keep warm.

Take the chicken out of the oven, baste and flip it over on to its breast very carefully, without breaking the skin. This will ensure the breast stays lovely and moist by keeping the juices sitting against it. Leave to rest for 15 minutes in a warm place.

Lift the bird from the pan and allow all the juices to run out of it back into the pan. Add a splash of water to the pan, place over a high heat and stir up the residue on the bottom to combine all the flavours together.

Strain this gravy and serve alongside your carved chicken with the carrots.

Glazed chicken wing pieces with crudités of spring vegetables

This simple way with the most inexpensive parts of the chicken makes a very quick and cheap light supper.

20 chicken wing pieces (breast knuckle bone, trimmed)

FOR THE MARINADE

Pinch of dried chilli flakes

1 teaspoon fennel seeds

Grated zest and juice of 1 lemon

2 tablespoons Worcestershire sauce

1 tablespoon Demerara sugar

2 tablespoons soy sauce

12 ripe tomatoes, chopped

2 tablespoons brown sauce, preferably HP

3 garlic cloves, crushed

FOR THE CRUDITÉS

Good handful of young carrots

Good handful of young fennel

Good handful of breakfast radishes

Good handful of cherry tomatoes

Good-quality olive oil for drizzling

Splash of lemon juice

Maldon sea salt

Freshly ground black pepper

The day before, make the marinade by mixing all the ingredients in a pan with 200ml water. Bring to the boil and simmer until thick. Strain through a fine sieve and leave to cool. When quite cool, add the chicken pieces, mix well to coat them and leave to marinate in the fridge overnight.

Next day, preheat the oven to 160°C/gas 3. Lift the chicken pieces out of the marinade, put on a roasting tray and bake until cooked through, about 20 minutes.

While the chicken is baking, prepare the vegetable crudités: trim the vegetables and cut them into bite-sized pieces if necessary, then dress them in the olive oil mixed with a splash of lemon juice and some Maldon sea salt and freshly ground black pepper.

Serve the cooked chicken alongside the crudités, together with some of the marinade that has been boiled up.

Fricassee of chicken legs with lyonnaise potatoes

Cooking the potatoes in their jackets helps prevent them from disintegrating when they are fried later.

6 whole chicken legs, cut into thighs and drumsticks

Good splash of vegetable oil

50g butter

1 large onion, finely chopped

3 garlic cloves, thinly sliced

2 bay leaves

Sprig of savory or thyme

100ml white wine vinegar

200ml white wine

500ml chicken stock or water

200ml double cream

1 tablespoon chopped flat-leaf parsley

FOR THE LYONNAISE POTATOES

6 large Maris Piper potatoes

Salt and freshly ground black pepper

125g butter

2 onions, thinly sliced

2 garlic cloves, crushed

2 tablespoons olive oil

Preheat the oven to 170°C/gas 3½.

Brown the chicken pieces in the vegetable oil and butter in a heavy-based casserole until nicely golden and caramelized.

While the chicken is browning, start preparing the lyonnaise potatoes: cook the unpeeled potatoes in gently simmering salted water until almost soft all the way through. Take out and leave to cool completely.

Take the chicken out of the casserole and reserve. Add the onion, garlic, bay and savory or thyme to the casserole, and cook until soft. Add the vinegar and reduce by two-thirds. Add the wine and reduce by half. Add the stock, cream and chicken pieces. Bring to the boil and skim off any scum.

Cook in the preheated oven for about 20 minutes.

When the potatoes are cold, peel them and cut into 1cm slices. In a large heavy sauté pan, melt half the butter and fry the onions and garlic until soft and golden. Season and set aside. Heat the remaining butter and olive oil, add the sliced potatoes and gently colour on both sides. Add the onion and garlic mix, adjust the seasoning and serve.

Take the chicken pieces out of the liquid and set aside. Bring the sauce back to the boil and finish by adding the parsley and adjusting the seasoning, if necessary.

Return the chicken to the sauce and serve with the potatoes.

Roast coquelet, spatchcock-style with a sauce of tender young garlic

I find coquelets, small young cockerels, to be very tender and succulent when cooked this way. Spatchcocking is a preparation that lends itself to the cooking of young chickens. The backbone is removed and the breastbone flattened to give a butterfly effect. They are then very quick to cook and not at all labour-intensive. One coquelet could serve two people, but one per person is much more satisfying and generous.

SERVES 4

4 heads of tender young garlic

Salt and freshly ground black pepper

4 coquelets or poussins (ask your butcher to spatchcock them for you)

4 tablespoons olive oil

2 tablespoons dried oregano

4 sprigs of thyme, picked

Grated zest and juice of 2 lemons

50g butter

Preheat the oven to 180°C/gas 4.

Break the bulbs of garlic into cloves. Peel one and reserve, leaving the skins on the others. Just cover these with cold salted water in a small pan and bring to the boil. Drain, refresh with cold water and drain again. Repeat this process twice more – this will make the garlic much more palatable.

Rub the peeled garlic clove over the birds and then liberally brush with olive oil. Season the oiled skin with salt, pepper, dried and fresh herbs, lemon juice and zest.

In a pan big enough to hold all the birds you are cooking (or do this in batches), heat the remaining olive oil and the butter, and brown the birds evenly to get them crisp all over. When all are nicely golden, roast in a large baking pan (or 2) for about 15–20 minutes, or until you can feel the meat come away from the thigh with just a little pressure.

When done, take from the oven and leave to rest in a warm place. The pan should hold a lot of juice; take this out and reserve. Add another slug of oil and knob of butter to the pan and sauté the blanched garlic until golden. This should have a crisp shell but meltingly soft inner. Add this tasty pulp to the chicken with the juices, adjust the seasoning and serve.

Chicken oysters *sot-y-laisse* with peas and macaroni

Prized by the French, who call them *sot-y-laisse*, meaning 'a fool would leave it', the oysters are the two tear-shaped succulent and tasty little bits of meat to be found behind the leg on the backbone of the bird, where it meets the thigh. As it lies on the underside of a trussed bird, it is even often missed by people carving a roast chicken. If your butcher sells ready-jointed chicken, then he may be able to supply you with oysters, which are otherwise discarded with the bones. If you can't get a hold of oysters, you could use the little underfillets from the breasts, which are now being sold in packs as 'mini fillets'. Cut these across in half or into three, depending on their length.

SERVES 4

150ml double cream

150ml chicken stock

Grated zest and juice of 1 lemon

2 garlic cloves

2 sprigs of rosemary

2 sprigs of summer savory

200g fresh macaroni

Salt and freshly ground black pepper

65g butter

20 chicken oysters (see above)

150g fresh peas, cooked

Put the cream, stock, lemon zest and juice, garlic, rosemary and savory in a pan, and simmer the mixture until reduced by half.

Cook the macaroni in a large pan of salted boiling water until al dente. Drain, refresh in cold water and set aside.

In a large frying pan, heat the butter and quickly sauté the chicken oysters until nicely caramelized. Add the pasta, cooked peas and the cream mixture, and toss together until well mixed and the pasta is well coated.

Finally, adjust the seasoning and serve.

beef & veal

ROAST RIB OF BEEF WITH FAT CHIPS * BEEF TARTARE * TRADITIONAL CORNED BEEF WITH SALSA VERDE * BRAISED JACOB'S LADDER WITH SHALLOTS À LA CRÈME * BRISKET POT AU FEU WITH TRADITIONAL ROOT VEGETABLES * OXTAIL RAVIOLI IN ITS OWN STOCK * BAVETTE OF BEEF WITH GRATIN DAUPHINOISE AND RED WINE AND SHALLOT SAUCE * VEAL BREAST AND SWISS CHARD PIE * CARAMELIZED VEAL CHOP SLOW-COOKED WITH ROAST PLUM TOMATOES AND GARLIC * SLOW-COOKED SHIN OF VEAL WITH ROAST BONE MARROW, BRAISED CELERY AND CARROTS * BLANQUETTE OF VEAL WITH SEASONAL VEGETABLES *

Roast rib of beef with fat chips

Ask the butcher to French-trim the beef or, if you feel adventurous, have a go yourself. All you need to do is scrape out the fat and meat from between the protruding bones so that the joint presents more elegantly. You need a very sharp knife for this and you can add the meat to the pan towards the end of cooking so that it helps give even more flavour to the pan juices. It is always best to allow your meat to come to room temperature before you cook it, otherwise the exterior will overcook before the centre is properly done.

The quality of the chips depends enormously on the type of potato used at that particular time of the year. Too much starch and they will colour too quickly; too floury and they will crumble. I find Maris Pipers or King Edwards to be the better options. It's also a good idea to speak to your grocer to see what he or she recommends.

SERVES 4

2 knobs of butter

Couple of splashes of olive oil

One 2-bone rib of beef (from the forequarter)

3 garlic cloves, well crushed with the flat of a heavy knife

FOR THE FAT CHIPS

8 large potatoes (see above)

Vegetable or groundnut oil, for frying

Salt and freshly ground black pepper

Well ahead, start by pre-cooking the chips: peel the potatoes, cut them into 1cm thick slices and then cut these into chips 1cm in section. Place in a pan of salted cold water, bring to the boil gradually, then simmer gently until cooked but still retaining the tiniest bit of bite. Gently lift out with a slotted spoon and place to dry on a kitchen cloth until cold.

Preheat the oven to 150°C/gas 2.

Melt a knob of the butter with a splash of the oil in a heavy-based roasting pan. Season the meat liberally all over. When the pan is very hot, brown the meat all over until beautifully coloured (this will take time, but the extra flavour is well worth the effort).

When coloured, remove the meat from the pan and discard the spent fats. Add another knob of butter and splash of olive oil with the crushed garlic. Put the beef back in the roasting pan and roast slowly in the preheated oven, basting frequently. Ideally you need to invest in a meat temperature probe for this kind of cooking, as accuracy is crucial. We aim for an internal temperature of 55°C, which takes about 55–60 minutes and produces rare/medium-rare beef.

When cooked, let the meat rest in the pan for about 20 minutes in a warm place. Don't cover, as this steams the meat and you lose that lovely crisp charred exterior.

While the beef is resting, finish the chips. Heat oil for deep-frying to 180–200°C and pop the potatoes into this carefully. Do not overcrowd the pan or you will reduce the oil temperature too drastically and the result will be greasy chips; if necessary, cook in batches. Fry until golden, about 8–10 minutes. Lift out and douse with salt.

Carve the rested beef into slices (do add extra seasoning as you carve) and serve with the lovely pan juices and the just-cooked chips.

Beef tartare

You could also mince the beef, but I find chopping by hand gives a better texture. The pieces should be no smaller than about 3mm dice. Some people do this with two knives, one in each hand. As the egg yolks are raw, use only the freshest from an impeccable source.

SERVES 4

360g finely chopped beef, excluding all fat (we use bavette, i.e. skirt steak)

1 tablespoon finely chopped shallots

1 tablespoon miniature capers

1 tablespoon finely chopped gherkins

2 tablespoons finely chopped parsley

½ teaspoon Tabasco sauce

1 tablespoon Dijon mustard

2 tablespoons tomato ketchup

2 teaspoons Worcestershire sauce

1 teaspoon olive oil

Salt and freshly ground black pepper

4 egg yolks

Toasted sourdough bread, to serve

FOR THE GARNISH (OPTIONAL)

Extra-virgin olive oil

Maldon sea salt

Paprika

In a large mixing bowl, combine together to an even mix all the ingredients apart from the egg yolks and bread. Do not be afraid to add more of the seasoning ingredients according to your taste.

Mould the tartare mixture into 4 round patties. (You can use a 10cm pastry cutter to mould the mixture into shape if you like, or even cling film.) Place a patty on each serving plate, make a slight hollow on the top and add an egg yolk.

Serve as soon as possible, with slices of toasted sourdough bread. If you like, drizzle the plate with a little oil here and there and sprinkle over some sea salt crystals and paprika.

Traditional corned beef with salsa verde

Corned beef – beef preserved in brine – is such a classic, but our ideas of it are now very coloured by the tinned version. To do the real thing at home, it is important to get the right balance between fat and meat, and this is my interpretation of how it should be done. Because it has been used by terrorists in bombmaking, saltpetre has disappeared from most chemists' shelves, but you might well be able to get it via your butcher or Internet suppliers.

2kg brisket of beef

1 carrot

1 onion, peeled and studded with cloves

1 celery stalk, halved

6 garlic cloves, peeled

1 bouquet garni

Good bread, toasted, to serve

FOR THE BRINE

200g sugar

200g salt

20g saltpetre

2 juniper berries

1 bay leaf

10 white peppercorns

FOR THE SALSA VERDE

Bunch of spring onions

⅓ cucumber, peeled and deseeded

2 green peppers, peeled and deseeded

1 tablespoon chopped capers

1 tablespoon chopped gherkin

1 tablespoon chopped mixed herbs, such as chervil, tarragon, parsley and chives

Good extra-virgin olive oil

Salt and freshly ground black pepper

At least 2½ days ahead, make the brine: put all the ingredients in a large pan with 2 litres of water. Bring to the boil, skim and simmer for 10 minutes. Allow to cool completely.

When the brine is completely cold, put the beef in it and leave to cure in the fridge for 48 hours.

At the end of this time, rinse the beef well under cold running water for about 20 minutes. Then put it in a large pan, just cover with cold water, add the vegetables, garlic and bouquet garni, and bring to the boil. Reduce the heat and simmer gently for about 3 hours, until the meat is tender to the touch.

Take the beef out of the liquid and set aside. Reduce the remaining stock by half and leave to cool.

When the beef is cool enough to handle, chop it into very small pieces. Now mix it with the stock, adjust the seasoning and put into a suitable crock pot or Kilner jar. Leave for at least a couple of days before using; it will keep in the fridge for up to a week.

Just before you want to serve, make the salsa verde: chop the spring onions not too thinly and dice the cucumber and peppers to about the same size as the pieces of onion. In a bowl, mix these together with the remaining ingredients, adding just enough oil to bind the mixture together and create a chunky-textured salsa. Season to taste.

Serve the corned beef with slices of good bread, toasted, and the salsa verde.

Braised Jacob's ladder (short rib of organic beef) with shallots à la crème

Short rib of beef is seldom, if ever, served in this country. I discovered it on a recent visit to the USA, in a restaurant serving its own version of modern bistro food.

SERVES 4–6

2 short ribs of beef (Jacob's ladders) or enough for 4–6 people

Flour for coating

A little vegetable oil

2 knobs of butter

1 large onion, chopped

2 large carrots, chopped

1 celery stalk, chopped

6 garlic cloves, finely chopped

4 tablespoons red wine vinegar

375ml port

375ml full-bodied red wine

1 bouquet garni

2 litres chicken stock

Salt and freshly ground black pepper

FOR THE SHALLOTS À LA CRÈME

100g butter

2 garlic cloves

Sprig of thyme

18 medium-sized shallots

150ml Madeira

150ml double cream

Cut the short ribs into individual ribs and coat in flour. Heat a heavy-based casserole with a film of oil and the knob of butter in it. Add the floured ribs and lightly brown on all sides. Reserve.

Add another knob of butter, followed by the vegetables and garlic, and lightly brown them.

Deglaze the pan with the vinegar and reduce by two-thirds. Then add the port and wine, and reduce them by half. Add the ribs, bouquet garni and stock, bring to the boil and skim. Season with salt and pepper, and simmer for about 2 hours, skimming from time to time.

Towards the end of this time, prepare the shallots: melt the butter in a sauté pan, add the garlic and thyme, followed by the shallots, and cook, stirring, until the shallots are golden. Add the Madeira and cook until that is reduced by half. Add the cream with 150ml water and salt and pepper to taste. Bring to the boil and simmer until the shallots are tender.

When the ribs are cooked, carefully take them out of the cooking liquid and reserve. Strain the liquid and vegetables through a fine sieve into a clean pan. Add the ribs, adjust the seasoning and bring back to the boil to serve, together with the shallots.

Brisket *pot au feu* with traditional root vegetables

The reason I put the meat into hot stock is that it then retains a lot more of its flavour instead of it all seeping out into the liquid. The stock will, of course, be well flavoured, but the meat done this way will also be quite delicious. The veal knuckle will enrich and also add great flavour to the stock. I like to thicken the stock at the end with the marrow from the bone.

2 carrots, halved

1 leek, sliced and well rinsed

2 large onions, peeled and halved

2 heads of garlic

Bouquet garni

Handful of Maldon sea salt

Handful of white peppercorns

3kg piece of brisket on the bone

1 knuckle of veal (containing the bone marrow)

FOR THE TRADITIONAL ROOT VEGETABLES

1kg mixed root vegetables, such as chervil root, parsley root, parsnip and turnips, peeled and cut into chunks

2 handfuls of small white potatoes, peeled and cut into chunks

Half fill a large saucepan with cold water and add the carrots, leek, onions, garlic, bouquet garni, salt and peppercorns. Bring to a simmer, then carefully place in the beef brisket and the veal, and cook very gently for 3–4 hours or until the brisket bones easily come away from the meat. Don't forget to skim from time to time, but don't skim all the fat away, just the grey matter (blood).

When the meat is cooked, turn off the heat and leave to cool completely. Lift out the beef, veal and vegetables, and reserve. Drain the stock, discarding any peppercorns and the bouquet garni. Return to the heat and add the mixed root vegetables and potatoes, and cook gently until these are soft. I find that if they are added at the beginning, the stock tastes too much of them and they become too mushy.

Now discard the bones, together with the veal knuckle (remembering to scoop out any remaining marrow and stir it into the stock to thicken it). Also trim away any excess pieces of fat. Slice the brisket into equal portions and serve with all the vegetables and stock.

Oxtail ravioli in its own stock

We serve oxtail in two forms at the restaurant – on the bone or stuffed. After braising we usually find that quite a lot of the meat has come away from the bone and is not ideal for serving as a whole piece, but it does make an excellent stuffing in ravioli or even tortellini. You will need a pasta machine to make this recipe.

70g butter

Splash of olive oil

Salt and freshly ground black pepper

1 large oxtail, cut into pieces through the joints

Flour for dusting

1 large carrot, peeled and finely chopped

1 onion, finely chopped

6 garlic cloves, chopped

1 bay leaf

Sprig of thyme

1 tablespoon runny honey

1 bottle of full-bodied red wine

60ml double cream

About 1 heaped tablespoon freshly grated Parmesan cheese, plus more to serve

1 tablespoon chopped flat-leaf parsley

FOR THE RAVIOLI PASTA

500g '00' (Italian doppio zero) flour

3 whole eggs, plus 2 extra egg yolks

About 2 teaspoons olive oil

Melt the butter with the oil in a heavy-based pan. Season the individual pieces of oxtail and lightly dust with the flour. Colour them in the butter and olive oil until browned all over. Lower the heat, add the vegetables, garlic and herbs, and continue to colour these. At this stage you could add a splash of water, firstly to lower the heat and secondly to emulsify all the fats and juices together.

When the vegetables are all golden in colour, add the honey and red wine, bring to the boil, cover with cold water, bring to the boil again, then cover and simmer gently for 2–2½ hours, or until the oxtail is tender – the meat should fall freely from the bone.

Take out and reserve the oxtail with about 200ml of the braising stock. Add the cream to the remaining stock and reduce until syrupy. Pick off the meat from the tail and put it back into the creamy sauce. Add Parmesan to taste and season again to taste with salt and pepper, and combine well. This is the filling for the ravioli – it shouldn't be too heavy or over-reduced. At the last minute, add the parsley and leave to cool completely until set. Ideally, this should be done in the refrigerator.

To make the ravioli, in a large mixing bowl, mix the flour, eggs and extra yolks with just enough of the oil to make a paste. Leave to rest for about 30 minutes.

Roll the pasta out in the pasta machine on successively narrower settings until you get to the number 1 setting, producing a long pasta sheet about 2mm thick. Lay this out on a floured surface.

When the filling is completely cold, spoon pieces of it about the size of a 50p piece over one long half of the sheet of pasta, allowing a space of 2.5cm between each. Spray lightly with water, then carefully fold over the other half of the pasta sheet and seal well around the filling to make into individual ravioli, ensuring that as little air as possible is trapped in with the filling. To get rid of any air that is trapped, puncture the pasta with a pin, press out the air and pinch the hole closed.

Cut between the mounds of filling with a pastry wheel or sharp knife to make the individual ravioli. Ideally cook them straight away to prevent them drying out.

(If you are unable to cook at that time or want to pre-prepare, blanch the ravioli briefly, refresh in cold water to cool them right down, drain well and toss in a little olive oil; they may then be kept in the fridge for a day or so before cooking.)

To cook them, bring a large pan of water to the boil, add salt and then plunge the ravioli into it for 3–5 minutes, until the pasta is al dente and the filling warm. Remove with a slotted spoon and toss in a little olive oil with seasoning to taste.

Serve with a little of the reserved beef sauce, some greens and grated Parmesan.

Bavette of beef with gratin dauphinoise and red wine and shallot sauce

For me, this is the archetypal French bistro dish, yet it is seldom found in the UK and, if it is, it can often be disappointing. There's no big secret, just buy good-quality beef and cook it briefly. It's never going to be as tender as fillet, but the flavour is knock-out. What's more, it's cheap. However, you do need a damn good gratin dauphinoise to accompany it.

In the restaurant kitchens, with precisely calibrated ovens, I cook dauphinoise at 130°C, but as domestic ovens vary so widely, here I've specified a safer 150°C. It is also difficult to be too exact with times, as so much depends on the potatoes' moisture content, which varies even between varieties as well as whether they're floury or waxy, and how old they are. So start testing after 1½ hours and keep cooking and testing until just this side of actually setting. It is then essential to allow it to rest for 10-15 minutes for the perfect consistency. Sautéed shredded spring or winter greens make a colourful addition too.

SERVES 6

100g butter, plus an extra knob to finish the sauce

Splash of vegetable oil

6 bavette (skirt) steaks, each about 200g

2 garlic cloves, crushed

Sprig of thyme

10 large shallots, finely chopped

300ml full-bodied red wine

Sautéed shredded spring or winter greens, to serve (optional)

FOR THE GRATIN DAUPHINOISE

1.5 kg large waxy potatoes, preferably Desiree

550ml double cream

450ml full-fat milk

15g salt

Freshly ground black pepper

1 tablespoon puréed or grated garlic, plus 1 peeled whole clove to rub the pot

20g butter

First prepare the gratin dauphinoise: preheat the oven to 150°C/gas2. Slice the potatoes about 3mm thick. Quickly rinse and pat quite dry. In a large pan, heat the cream, milk, salt and pepper with the puréed/grated garlic until just below simmering. Toss in the potato slices and mix well. Rub a suitable earthenware, cast iron or stainless steel pot or deep baking dish with the whole garlic clove. Turn the pan contents into this dish, trying to ensure that all the potato slices are in layers and not sticking up. Dot the surface with the butter and bake for 1½ hours. Test by inserting a cocktail stick into the gratin. It should still feel barely liquid and wobble when shaken but not be too sloppy: if still too liquid, cook for another 15 minutes and test again. The surface should glaze nicely; if not you can finish it off under a hot grill. Do let it rest for 10-15 minutes before being served, so that it will achieve the right consistency.

About 20 minutes before the gratin will be ready, prepare the steaks. Heat 60g butter and a splash of vegetable oil in a large frying pan. Season the steaks and sear in the butter and oil over a high heat until nicely browned on both sides. Tip half of this darkened oil and butter away. Then add the remaining butter with the garlic and thyme, and season again. Lower the heat a little and cook the steaks for about 4 minutes on each side, basting frequently.

When cooked, lift on to warmed serving plates and keep warm. Add the shallots to the pan with the red wine, increase the heat and reduce by two-thirds. Pour in the juice that has seeped from the cooked steaks, add a knob of butter, season to taste and pour over the meat.

Serve the steaks with the gratin and the greens if you are serving them.

Veal breast and Swiss chard pie

Illustrated on previous pages

Veal breast is a huge favourite with us and benefits enormously from slow cooking, braising or being used in a pie filling as here. I particularly favour dishes like this as they are so conducive to a convivial gathering around the dining table.

1 onion, chopped

2 carrots, chopped

4 garlic cloves, sliced

Sprig of rosemary

50g butter

2 tablespoons good olive oil

600g cooked veal breast, diced, and its juices (see the recipe for Slow-cooked shin of veal on page 98)

4 medium stalks of Swiss chard, cut into pieces and blanched

Salt and freshly ground black pepper

FOR THE PASTRY

200g flour

2 pinches of salt

A little chilled water

120g butter, cubed and chilled

1 egg, beaten

About 5 hours ahead, in a large heatproof pie dish or deep pan, sweat the onion, carrots, garlic and rosemary in the butter and olive oil. Add the veal and its juices with the chard. Season to taste, let cool and then refrigerate.

To make the pastry, place the flour and salt in a chilled stainless-steel bowl, add the butter and mash with a fork, working quickly so the butter doesn't melt. Bring the mixture into the middle of the bowl and make a well (all with the fork – hands are too hot). Add the chilled water to the well little by little to create a manageable paste (not too wet or dry). Quickly create a ball with your fingertips, then refrigerate for 2 hours.

Roll out the pastry on a lightly floured surface to a thickness of just under about 1cm. Place on top of veal mix, press to seal at the edges and let rest for another hour in the fridge.

Preheat the oven to 180°C/gas 4.

Brush the top of the pastry with the beaten egg, make a hole in the centre to allow steam to vent and bake in the preheated oven for 10 minutes to set the pastry. Lower the oven setting to 160°C/gas 3 and continue to cook until nicely golden, about 15–20 minutes.

Caramelized veal chop slow-cooked with roast plum tomatoes and garlic

This won't be a cheap dish to make, so definitely keep it for a special occasion. It is very simple to cook but it is crucially important that you caramelize the meat correctly and ideally serve it medium rare. This is my own favourite restaurant dish.

SERVES 4

120g butter, plus an extra knob to finish

3 tablespoons olive oil

4 veal chops, French-trimmed (we only use ethical English or French rosé veal)

2 sprigs of lemon thyme or winter savory

Juice of 1 lemon

FOR THE ROAST PLUM TOMATOES AND GARLIC

8–10 plum tomatoes, preferably still on the vine

2–3 heads of garlic, separated into cloves and blanched as described on page 74

Splash of olive oil

Salt and freshly ground black pepper

First prepare the roast plum tomatoes and garlic: preheat the oven to 125°C/gas ¾. Score the bottom of the tomatoes as if you were skinning them. Liberally coat them and the blanched garlic with olive oil, salt and pepper and roast in the preheated oven for about 1 hour.

Meanwhile, in a heavy-based pan, bring the butter and oil to foaming point. Season the chops, add them to the pan and caramelize over a high heat, 5–10 minutes (this is crucial for the flavour of the meat).

When coloured, reduce heat to low, add the herbs and continue to cook until the chops are firm to the touch, about 10 minutes for medium – cook veal only to medium to avoid it becoming dry!

Lift out the chops and pour away the butter but reserve the herbs. Put the chops back into the pan and leave to rest in a warm place – they will ooze some juices during this period.

To serve, arrange the chops on serving plates, add a knob of butter to the pan, re-boil with the herbs, a squeeze of lemon juice, and salt and pepper. Pour over the chops.

Serve the chops with the roast tomatoes and garlic.

Slow-cooked shin of veal with roast bone marrow, braised celery and carrots

This is possibly one of the most classic bistro dishes we serve as, apart from veal chops, shin is the best and tastiest veal cut. Make sure you get cuts of shin that reveal the marrow, which is crucial to the final dish.

SERVES 4–6

2 large shins of veal (ideally French or English), short cut

200g butter

2 whole heads of garlic, broken down into cloves, peeled and halved

2 sprigs of rosemary

Grated zest and juice of 1 lemon, plus more juice to serve

8 good-quality anchovy fillets

375ml full-bodied white wine

1 tablespoon extra-virgin olive oil

FOR THE BRAISED VEGETABLES

100 unsalted butter

1 garlic clove, crushed

Sprig of rosemary

2 bunches of young carrots about 5cm long

1 bunch of celery, strings peeled off and cut into 5cm lengths

250ml Madeira

Salt and freshly ground black pepper

Preheat the oven to 155–170°C/gas 2–3.

In a heavy-based ovenproof pan (I find cast-iron pans best for this) over a moderate heat, brown the shins in half the butter until they are a deep gold colour.

Take out the shins and discard the blackened butter. Add the remaining butter and cook until nut-brown. Add the shins back, together with the garlic, rosemary, lemon zest and juice, and the anchovies. Finally, add the wine and water to a depth of 2.5cm. Cover and cook in the preheated oven, basting and turning the meat every 15–20 minutes, and topping up the water, if necessary, for about 2 hours. The meat should easily come away from the bone and yield under pressure.

Towards the end of this time, prepare the braised vegetables. Melt the butter in a heavy-based casserole with the garlic and rosemary, then colour the vegetables in this mixture until golden. Add the Madeira and reduce by half, then add a few spoonfuls of the veal cooking liquid and 250ml water. Cover and simmer until the vegetables are tender and nicely glazed. Season well.

When the veal is cooked, spoon the marrow out of the bones and add to the cooking juices. Boil to reduce to a rich gravy and finish with a tablespoon of extra-virgin olive oil and a squeeze of lemon juice.

Serve with the braised vegetables.

Blanquette of veal with seasonal vegetables

I find that breast of veal is the best cut for this dish, which is one which we often serve at Arbutus. Its cartilaginous texture and silky richness lend themselves to slow cooking, which produces incomparable results. If you have trouble finding the breast, belly or shoulder is a good alternative. Traditional recipes tell us to blanch the veal first, but I find this eradicates a lot of the delicate flavour and all impurities will be strained off at a later stage.

1kg veal breast (preferably English rose or French Limousin), cut into large dice about 2.5cm square

2.5 litres chicken stock

6 garlic cloves, peeled and crushed

1 teaspoon black peppercorns

Salt and freshly ground black pepper

Sprig of sage

1 bay leaf

Finely grated zest and juice of 1 lemon

6 medium potatoes, such as Maris Piper, peeled, cut in half and trimmed

2 bunches of young carrots

2 medium leeks, well rinsed and cut into 2.5cm lozenges

Handful of spring greens (any firm green leaf, like cabbage or cavolo nero, will do)

50g butter

50g flour

1 tablespoon chopped parsley

50ml whipping cream, whipped to soft peaks

Put the diced veal in a saucepan, cover with the stock and bring to the boil. Reduce to a simmer and skim all the scum from the surface. Add the garlic, peppercorns, salt (not too much), sage, bay leaf and lemon zest. Continue to simmer gently for about 1 hour.

Add the potatoes, carrots, leeks and greens, and cook until these are soft. They will cook at different stages, so lift them out when ready and leave to cool naturally. By now the veal should be tender or just yield under pressure; if so, lift it out and allow to cool naturally. Keep the stock simmering.

In another pan, ideally the same size, melt the butter until foaming (noisette), then add the flour and stir to make a roux (making the roux with noisette butter gives a great nutty taste to the stock). Now strain the simmering stock into the roux, stirring constantly. Lower the heat and simmer for 20–30 minutes, to allow the flour to cook thoroughly. Adjust the seasoning with salt and pepper, and lemon juice. Add the meat, vegetables and parsley, then finish by stirring in the cream to serve.

lamb

ARBUTUS SHEPHERD'S PIE ❧ SLOW-COOKED BREAST OF LAMB, SWEETBREADS AND GOLDEN SULTANAS ❧ RUMP OF LAMB AND BROAD BEANS WITH CRUSHED JERSEY ROYALS ❧ SLOW-COOKED SHOULDER OF ELWY VALLEY LAMB ❧ SAUTÉ OF LAMB NECK FILLET WITH ARTICHOKES ❧ ROAST LEG OF SALT-MARSH LAMB IN A SALT CRUST ❧ GIGOT OF LAMB WITH ROAST BRANDYWINE TOMATOES ❧ NAVARIN OF SPRING LAMB AND VEGETABLES ❧

Arbutus shepherd's pie

This is a typical *plat du jour* dish which goes down very well at the restaurant during the spring and summer seasons. As we buy whole animals, we have lots of different lamb cuts around the kitchen. This shepherd's pie is our way of gathering up what's in the kitchen on a particular day. Instead of cooking with butter and olive oil, you could use lamb fat, as it has such a wonderful flavour. The great thing about a dish like this is that it can be made a couple of days in advance.

50g butter, plus more for dotting

Splash of olive oil

1 onion, finely chopped

2 carrots, diced

1 teaspoon chopped lemon thyme

1 teaspoon chopped rosemary

4 garlic cloves, puréed

4 tomatoes, skinned, deseeded and diced

2 handfuls of peas, blanched

500ml lamb stock (juices from the braised lamb on page 106)

Salt and freshly ground black pepper

1kg cooked lamb – breast, shoulder and shanks (see the recipes on the subsequent pages), diced

Potato purée (see page 131)

Melt the butter with the oil in a large heavy-based pot and cook the onion, carrots, thyme and rosemary until the vegetables take on a little colour, then add the garlic, tomatoes, peas and lamb stock. Bring to the boil, simmer and season. Cook until the vegetables are soft. When cooked, take off the heat and leave to go cold.

When cold, preheat the oven to 160°C/gas 3. Mix your roughly diced lamb meat into the cold vegetables and combine well. This is now ready to go into your pie dish or roasting pot. Top the meat and vegetables with potato purée, dot with butter and bake for about 45 minutes, or until hot and golden.

Slow-cooked breast of lamb, sweetbreads and golden sultanas

Get the butcher to remove the bones from the lamb breast, but do ask him to save them as you will need them for the cooking liquor. It is important here to use a pan that is just the right size to hold the lamb breasts; it can't be too big, otherwise the braising stock will be very dilute and so won't have much flavour.

2 breasts of lamb, bones removed but reserved

8 garlic cloves, puréed.

2 sprigs of rosemary, finely chopped

Salt and freshly ground black pepper

100g butter

Couple of splashes of olive oil

2 onions, thinly sliced

1 teaspoon fennel seeds

1 teaspoon herbes de Provence

200ml dry white wine

FOR THE LAMB SWEETBREADS

Knob of butter

Splash of olive oil

200g lamb sweetbreads, blanched and outer membrane removed

1 teaspoon honey

1 tablespoon balsamic vinegar

Handful of golden sultanas

Preheat the oven to 150°C/gas 2.

Smear the flesh side of the breasts with the garlic, rosemary, salt and pepper. Roll the breasts and tie them so they each resemble a Swiss roll, the skin side outwards.

In a pan just big enough to hold them and which also has a tight-fitting lid, melt 50g of the butter with a splash of olive oil. Colour the breast rolls in this until nicely golden all over. this could take 15 minutes or so, and the slower it is done the better, as this helps render the fat needed for the next stage. Take out the lamb and set it aside.

Add the sliced onions, fennel seeds and herbes de Provence, and cook until the onions are very soft, about 15 minutes.

Place the breasts back in the pan on top of the onions, then add the wine, lamb bones and enough water to come halfway up the lamb. Lightly season the breasts, put the cover on, pop into the preheated oven and cook for about 2 hours or more. The lamb should be tender to the touch. Lift the breasts out and keep in a warm place until needed.

Reduce the braising stock until you have about 200ml. Strain through a fine sieve, pushing all the juices from the onions, etc. through. Set aside.

While the breasts are resting, prepare the lamb sweetbreads. In a non-stick pan, melt the remaining butter with a splash of olive oil. Increase the heat and sauté the seasoned lamb sweetbreads until golden. Add the honey and caramelize a little, then add the vinegar, followed by the sultanas and 50ml of braising stock. Toss the sweetbreads and sultanas together; this will coat and glaze everything. Taste and adjust the seasoning, if necessary, and serve alongside the breasts.

With this dish we serve a vegetable purée, such as the root vegetable purée on page 59, and some sautéed seasonal greens.

Rump of lamb and broad beans with crushed Jersey Royals

To me this dish typifies the late spring months. We use rump as we find that it usually has better flavour than the best end – and is significantly cheaper. The crushed Jersey Royals laced with olive oil complement it superbly.

SERVES 4

4 lamb rumps, each about 250g

Salt and freshly ground black pepper

Knob of butter

Splash of olive oil

FOR THE CRUSHED JERSEY ROYALS

500g Jersey Royal potatoes, unpeeled

Knob of butter

Splash of olive oil

FOR THE BROAD BEANS

4 shallots, finely chopped

70g butter

100ml Riesling white wine

50ml whipping cream

300g broad beans (shelled weight), blanched and peeled

3 sprigs of marjoram, chopped

Preheat the oven to 160°C/gas 3.

Season the lamb all over. Melt the butter with the olive oil in a frying pan and lightly colour the flesh side of the rumps in it. Turn over on to the skin side and finish roasting in the preheated oven for about 10 minutes for a medium-rare result. Allow to rest for about 10 minutes.

While the lamb is roasting and resting, cook the Jersey Royals in gently boiling salted water. Drain and peel while still warm. Put in a stainless-steel bowl, add a knob of butter, drizzle with olive oil, season and crush with a fork or old-fashioned potato masher, adding more butter and olive oil as you go. The aim is to create a homogeneous texture. The quantities of olive oil should be greater than the butter. The potatoes should be rich but also have hints of fruitiness from the oil. Keep warm.

While the potatoes are cooking, prepare the broad beans. Sweat the shallots in the butter until soft, add the wine and cook until syrupy. Add the cream, beans and marjoram. Season with salt and pepper and simmer for 5–10 minutes.

Serve the rested lamb with the roasting pan juices and the potatoes and broad beans.

Slow-cooked shoulder of Elwy Valley lamb

Shoulder is without doubt the best-flavoured of all the lamb joints. Cooked slowly in this way and served at room temperature, there can be few more satisfying pieces of meat. Elwy Valley lamb is a favourite with many restaurateurs, as it continually comes top of comparative tastings. Farmed up to 1,000 feet in the Welsh mountains, in view of the Snowdonia range, the lambs are raised to both animal welfare and environmentally friendly standards.

Salt and freshly ground black pepper

1 lamb shoulder, preferably Elwy Valley, weighing about 2.5kg

100g butter

50 ml olive oil

4 onions, thinly sliced

15 garlic cloves, thinly sliced

2 sprigs of summer or winter savory

2 bay leaves

400ml white wine

Preheat the oven to 120°C/gas ½. For this recipe you will need a roasting tray or deep cast-iron pot which has a tight-fitting lid. In it, colour the seasoned lamb shoulder all over in the butter and olive oil. Take out and set aside.

Do not pour away the fat, but add the onions, garlic and herbs, and lightly colour. Pour in the white wine and bring to the boil. Reduce to a simmer and return the lamb to the tray or pot. Season it again with salt and pepper. Cover and place in the preheated oven and slow-bake for about 4–5 hours, basting frequently. The pot must not dry out, so add a splash of water if necessary at any point.

When the lamb is tender, turn the oven setting up to about 180°C/gas 4, lift the cover off and continue to bake for about another 15 minutes, which will crisp up the lamb skin. Remove from the oven.

Leave to cool until just warm – I think that this is the best temperature to serve this dish. It goes really well with the Stuffed tomatoes 'Greek style' (see page 160) or the English peas with lettuce and bacon (see page 147).

Sauté of lamb neck fillet with artichokes

The neck is probably the most underutilized part of the animal and consequently most of it is sold to the donner kebab industry. Interestingly, our lamb supplier tells us that we are the only restaurant on their books that takes the neck fillet. Again, it is incredibly cheap and packed with flavour – and not as scary to use as it sounds. It is best marinated and then grilled or sautéed.

SERVES 4

4 lamb neck fillets

Splash of olive oil

FOR THE MARINADE

2 garlic cloves, crushed

Sprig of mint

Sprig of rosemary

1 teaspoon fennel seeds

Pinch of chilli flakes

10 black peppercorns, crushed

Salt and freshly ground black pepper

2 tablespoons pineapple juice

100ml olive oil

FOR THE GARNISH

4 cooked globe artichokes, including the stalks

8 cherry tomatoes, scored at the bottom

Celery leaves (optional)

The day before, make the marinade by first combining all the dry ingredients to a paste using a pestle and mortar, then add the wet ingredients and mix well. Rub the lamb neck fillets in this and allow to marinate overnight in the fridge.

Next day, lift the lamb out of the marinade and set aside; reserve the marinade. Heat a splash of olive oil in a frying pan and colour the lamb briskly on a high heat until golden all over. Lower the heat, add a spoonful of the marinade to the pan and continue to cook for about 5 minutes more on each side.

Take the lamb out of the pan, season with salt and allow to rest in a warm to place.

To prepare the garnish, pop the cut artichokes in the pan and lightly colour. Add the tomatoes and blister the skins over high heat. Now add the juices from the rested lamb, one more spoonful of the marinade and cook on a low heat for 2 minutes.

Slice the lamb, pop it back in the pan and coat with all the juices to serve. If you have celery leaves, dot them around.

Roast leg of salt-marsh lamb in a salt crust

I believe this method of cooking originated in China. It is a great way of avoiding moisture loss, while retaining all the essential flavour from the meat and seasoning. The cooking time may look short, but with this method you have little heat loss if the crust is airtight as the steam released from the meat is retained in the stone-like crust.

1 leg of lamb, preferably salt-marsh, about 2.5kg

8 garlic cloves, peeled and split, any green germ removed

2 sprigs of rosemary, picked

Salt and freshly ground black pepper

Olive oil

FOR THE SALT CRUST

1kg ordinary table salt

1kg flour, plus more for dusting

1 egg, beaten

A little Maldon or rock salt

Handful of herbes de Provence

Prick the lamb deeply here and there all over with a small sharp knife and insert the garlic and rosemary into the holes. Season well and then colour the lamb all over in the olive oil until nicely golden. Season again and leave to go cold.

Preheat the oven to 200°C/gas 6.

To make the salt crust, mix the table salt and flour together, then add just enough water to bind to a pliable dough. Allow to rest for 5–10 minutes.

Roll the pastry out, liberally dusting it with flour, until big enough to enrobe the lamb completely. Place the lamb inside and completely wrap, sealing with egg wash as you go. Brush all over the outside with egg and, for a better presentation, dust the top with a little Maldon or rock salt and some dried herbs. Bake in the preheated oven for 15 minutes – this will set the paste immediately. Turn the oven setting down to 180°C/gas 4 and roast for a further 1½ hours.

Take the lamb out of the oven and leave undisturbed for 20 minutes.

With a serrated knife, cut around the crust to open the top – ideally this should be done in front of your guests, so the salty, garlicky, herby aromas combine with the smell of the lamb… Heavenly!

Gigot of lamb with roast Brandywine tomatoes

Gigot or leg steak is one of my favourite cuts of lamb. Whether it's cooked over a searing char-grill or in a pan, it's a great way to celebrate the arrival of the new season's lamb. I find Welsh lamb is the tastiest – maybe because they have so much lush green grass on which to graze. Whatever it is, the farmers are doing something right. June or July is also the best month for lamb because, being older, it has by then developed more flavour and goes well with these great roast tomatoes.

SERVES 4

Maldon salt and freshly ground black pepper

4 leg steaks

100ml good olive oil

FOR THE ROAST TOMATOES

1kg Brandywine tomatoes, or another heirloom variety, blanched, skinned and halved

4 sprigs of lemon thyme

Splash of olive oil

Splash of good-quality balsamic vinegar

Preheat a hot griddle or frying pan. Season the steaks well and drizzle with olive oil, then fry/griddle over a fierce heat until nicely coloured. I prefer the steaks to be charred on the outside and tender and pink in the middle. You will need to gauge this yourself, but allow about 3 minutes on each side. Touch and prod the meat to judge the cooking degree. Take from the heat and allow to rest.

To prepare the roast tomatoes, colour them in the same pan as the steaks over the same fierce heat with the lemon thyme. Season with Maldon salt, pepper and add a splash each of olive oil and balsamic vinegar to the pan.

Finish by adding the juices from the now rested lamb to the pan and serve immediately.

Navarin of spring lamb and vegetables

This is a modern lighter interpretation of the classic dish in which a prime cut of lamb is left pink and tender.

SERVES 4–6

4 (middle) necks of lamb

Salt and freshly ground black pepper

4 tablespoons olive oil

Bunch of young carrots

Bunch of young turnips

Bunch of young leeks, trimmed and well rinsed

2 handfuls of peeled young potatoes

Handful of podded fresh peas

Handful of podded and skinned broad beans

1 litre full-flavoured lamb stock

2 garlic cloves

Sprig of rosemary

Sprig of lemon thyme

Cut each neck into pieces about 2.5cm thick, aiming to get 4–5 pieces from each. Season with salt and pepper, drizzle with half the oil and set aside.

Cook the vegetables whole in the stock with the garlic and herbs. They will cook at different rates, so cook each vegetable individually, removing them with a slotted spoon when tender.

When they are all cooked, boil the stock rapidly to reduce it to a consistency that will coat the back of a spoon and set aside.

Heat 2 tablespoons of olive oil in a large casserole or deep frying pan and sauté the pieces of lamb over a highish heat until golden all over. Add the vegetables and reduced stock, bring back to the boil and serve.

pork

ROAST LOIN OF PORK WITH CRUSHED POTATOES ❧ FARMHOUSE TERRINE WITH DAMSON CHEESE ❧ CRISP BELLY OF PORK WITH LENTILS AND GRANNY SMITH APPLE PURÉE ❧ PIG'S CHEEK, EAR AND TROTTER SALAD WITH CRISP BARLEY ❧ BRAISED PIG'S HEAD, POTATO PURÉE, CARAMELIZED ONIONS AND ANDOUILLE ❧ PORK AND CABBAGE 'CAILLETTES' (MEATBALLS) ❧ SMOKED HAM HOCK, POTATO, PARSLEY AND SHALLOT SALAD WITH MUSTARD DRESSING ❧ CLASSIC ENGLISH BRAWN WITH HOMEMADE PICCALILLI ❧ POTTED PORK, BACON AND CABBAGE

Roast loin of pork with crushed potatoes

You will see that I recommend cooking the pork only until it is just still barely pink to avoid drying it out. Fortunately the days of worrying about pink pork are almost entirely gone, as better welfare on pig farms has led to the virtual elimination of the trichinosis parasite. Pigs are also now bred to be much leaner – almost to the detriment of the pork – so dryness is much more of a concern.

1 (6-bone) loin of pork (not too fatty)

Handful of Maldon salt, crushed

Freshly ground black pepper

Splash of vegetable oil

A few drops of lemon juice (optional)

FOR THE CRUSHED POTATOES

8 large Maris Piper potatoes, unpeeled

Salt

Knob of butter

2 onions, diced and cooked in butter

2 garlic cloves, crushed

Well ahead, start preparing the potatoes. Put them, unpeeled, in a pan of salted water and bring to the boil, then simmer very gently until almost cooked through. Leave to cool.

Preheat the oven to 170°C/gas 3½.

Score the rind on the pork equally between the cutlet bones down towards the meat so that each chop has a good piece of fat. Rub the salt and pepper all over the rind, getting it in between the incisions. Leave at room temperature for 15 minutes to allow the seasonings to penetrate.

Heat the vegetable oil in a roasting pan until very hot. Add the pork, skin side down, and start to crisp the rind. This will take 5–10 minutes. Then lift the pork upright, so the bones are sticking up, and roast in the preheated oven for about 40 minutes. Pork can be eaten slightly pink (see above), which stops it being tough and dry. Remove the pork from the roasting pan and allow to rest in a warm place for about 15 minutes.

Towards the end of the pork cooking time, peel the now-cool potatoes and cut them into slices 1cm thick. Sauté these slices in hot butter until golden and crisp around the edges. Add the cooked onions and garlic, and continue to sauté until potatoes are crisp all over. Now crush the potatoes with a fork and continue to sauté until they resemble crushed roast potatoes. Season and serve.

Add a splash of water to the roasting pan, put over a high heat and scrape the sediment with a wooden spoon. Season with salt and pepper, and possibly a few drops of lemon juice.

Serve the chops with some of this pan-gravy and the crushed potatoes.

Farmhouse terrine with damson cheese

Fruit cheeses, like this damson cheese, are nothing to do with dairy products, but are a rich reduction of the fruit so solid it can be sliced like a cheese. The damson is a small oval type of plum with a very high acid content that makes their flavour just a little too tart, but they do lend themselves to this sort of treatment. You'll need a large terrine dish about 1.5 litres in capacity.

600g smoked streaky bacon (or enough to line a large terrine)

Knob of butter

Splash of olive oil

300g onions, finely chopped

20g garlic, puréed

4g ground allspice

30ml Madeira

60ml port

650g minced pork

115g smoked back bacon, minced

225g chicken livers, minced

200g pork back fat, minced

2 eggs, lightly beaten

2g chopped rosemary

10g whole green peppercorns

5g salt

Good crusty bread, to serve

FOR THE DAMSON CHEESE

500g damsons

Zest and juice of 1 lemon

Zest and juice of 1 orange

250g sugar

Ideally make the terrine at least 3 days before you want to serve it. Preheat the oven to 110°C/gas ¼ with a bain-marie of hot water in it (a deep roasting tin half-filled with hot water will be fine).

Line a large terrine with foil and then with the bacon, leaving sufficient overhang to cover the top eventually.

Melt the butter with the oil in a frying pan and gently sweat the onions, garlic and allspice until soft, then leave to cool.

Mix the Madeira and port together in a pan and boil to reduce by two-thirds. Leave to cool.

Mix all the minced meats and fat with the eggs to bind, then mix in the cool onions and cool wine reduction, the rosemary, peppercorns and salt. Use to fill the lined terrine, making sure to pack the mixture in as compactly as possible. Give it a good whack on a chopping board to disperse any trapped air. Fold the bacon over to cover the mix and finally cover with overlapping foil.

Bake in the bain-marie in the preheated oven for about 80 minutes or until the centre of the terrine reaches 70°C. Take out of the bain-marie and leave to cool at room temperature. Ideally leave in the fridge or a cool place for 3 days before using to give the flavours a chance to develop.

To make the damson cheese, put the damsons in a large heavy-based pan with 200ml water and the citrus zests and juices. Cover and slowly stew until soft, about 20–30 minutes. Pass through a mouli or sieve, discarding the stones and stems. Return the pulp to the rinsed-out pan, add the sugar and stir well to combine. Bring gradually to the boil, skim and simmer gently until it looks as if it will set firm when cooled (pop a small amount on a plate and chill briefly to see if it's setting). When ready, pour into sterilized jars or moulds and let it go completely cold, then cover and store in a cool place. It will keep for 2–3 months in the fridge.

Serve the terrine cut into thick slices, with the damson cheese and good crusty bread.

Crisp belly of pork with lentils and Granny Smith apple purée

I favour apples with a high acidity, like Granny Smiths, to cut through the fattiness of the pork belly. If you can't get apples that are sufficiently acidic, you can always add a little lemon juice to the purée.

1 pork belly, about 1.5kg

1 recipe quantity brine (see page 84)

2 heads of garlic

2 sprigs of thyme

Olive oil

Salt and freshly ground black pepper

FOR THE LENTILS

25g butter

2 carrots, diced

2 celery stalks, strings removed and diced

2 onions, peeled and diced

300g Puy lentils

FOR THE GRANNY SMITH APPLE PURÉE

4 Granny Smith apples

25g butter

The day before, using a craft knife, slash the pork rind into 1cm strips, making sure that you do not penetrate the meat. Place in the cooled brine for 1 day. This process not only flavours the meat, but also helps release water from the fat and rind, creating a base for fantastic crispy crackling.

Next day, take the pork from the brine, place in a pan of cold water, bring to the boil, lift out the pork and leave to cool slightly. Preheat the oven to 160°C/gas 3.

Place the garlic and thyme on the base of a roasting tray, put the pork on top, rind side up, and liberally drizzle with olive oil and salt. Pour 2cm of water into the tray, put in the preheated oven and roast for 1½–2 hours, topping up with water now and again just to stop it drying out.

When cooked, take from the oven and leave to cool down. Pour off all the juices and reserve. Place a tray or board on top of the pork and apply 3–4 plates to press and reshape the pork in order to obtain a nice flat appearance (otherwise it develops an odd shape during cooking and cooling).

To cook the lentils, melt the butter in a large heavy-based pan and lightly sweat the diced vegetables in it. Add the lentils and reserved juices from the pork. Top up with water to cover plus 2.5cm, bring to the boil and simmer until the lentils are cooked, about 30 minutes.

To make the Granny Smith apple purée, peel, core and chop the apples. Put in a stainless-steel pan with the butter, cover and cook over a low heat until soft, about 10–15 minutes. Crush or blend to a paste.

Serve the pork carved thickly, with the purée and lentils, while still warm.

Pig's cheek, ear and trotter salad with crisp barley

The crisp barley is an optional extra, but it does give the dish a great texture. Grilled rapeseed oil has a lovely nutty flavour; if you can't find any, just use a good olive oil.

2 pigs' ears

1 pig's trotter, split

12 pigs' cheeks, split

Couple of splashes of grilled rapeseed oil or olive oil, plus more for the barley if using it

200ml dry sherry

1 teaspoon chopped sage

2 shallots, diced

3 tablespoons chopped parsley

Salt and freshly ground black pepper

1 Granny Smith apple, peeled and chopped

2 kohlrabi, peeled and chopped into chunks

Knob of butter

4 tablespoons pearl barley (optional)

Preheat the oven to 160°C/gas 3.

In an ovenproof casserole, sauté the ears, trotter and cheeks in a splash of rapeseed oil until golden. Add 1 litre of water and the sherry, cover and cook in the preheated oven for about 3 hours.

When cooked, strain, reserving the liquid, and leave to cool.

Chop the pork coarsely, and add the sage, shallots, parsley and salt and pepper. Shape into 2 or 3 long cylinders using cling film tied at both ends and chill until set, about 4 hours.

Put the apple and kohlrabi in a saucepan with a knob of butter and a splash of water. Cover and simmer until soft. Liquidize to a purée.

If using it, cook the pearl barley in salted water until soft. Drain and dry on kitchen towel, then sauté in the grilled rapeseed oil until crisp.

Unwrap the pork cylinders and slice them into 2–3cm pieces. Heat another splash of oil in a frying pan and colour the pork pieces over a fairly high heat.

Serve 2 pieces of the pork mixture on each plate with some of the apple and kohlrabi purée, a scattering of the crisp barley, if using it, and some colourful baby leaves.

Braised pig's head, potato purée, caramelized onions and andouille

Good mashed potato depends on several factors. First, the right type of potato: it must be a floury variety – we always use Desiree. Second, you should bake the potatoes, not boil them. Third, they should be sieved quickly while they are still hot – this will burn your fingers, but that's a good sign. Finally, they should be combined with the warm milk and butter immediately after being sieved. At the restaurant, or even at home, I use a vegetable mouli placed on top of a combination of warm full-fat milk and salted butter. As they are sieved, they fall into the liquid, allowing no time to cool.

You can buy *andouille* – a French country sausage made from chitterlings and pork stomach – from any French butcher or, indeed, most good butchers. If they don't stock them, they should be able to get them for you. You will probably have quite a lot left over, but it is wonderful in salads.

2 pigs' heads, split

Salt and freshly ground black pepper

300ml red wine

5 shallots, finely chopped

4 tablespoons chopped parsley

1 large andouille

FOR THE CARAMELIZED ONIONS

70g butter

6 onions, thinly sliced

50g sugar

100ml red wine vinegar

FOR THE POTATO PURÉE

1kg floury potatoes, such as Desiree, unpeeled

About 200ml milk, warmed

100g butter

About 3 days ahead, soak the pigs' heads in lightly salted water for 12 hours to remove the blood.

Drain and singe the heads with a blowtorch to remove any hairs. Place in an ovenproof dish, skin side down. Preheat the oven to 110°C/gas ¼. Cover the heads with the wine, shallots and 1 litre water. Cover with a close-fitting lid and braise in the oven for 8 hours. Remove the heads from the liquid and let cool. Skim the liquid and boil to reduce by half or until syrupy.

When the heads are cool enough to handle, remove and discard the bones, eyes and brain, and carefully set the meat aside. Remove the ears and slice them thinly. Combine the meat, ears, parsley, salt, pepper and reduced braising liquid. Set in a terrine or loaf tin lined with cling film. Leave for a couple of days to set and ripen.

To make the caramelized onions, melt the butter in a frying pan and gently colour the onions. Add the sugar and caramelize. Add the vinegar and reduce until almost dry. Add some salt and pepper, a splash of water and cook gently until onions are soft and jammy. Preheat the oven to 180°C/gas 4.

While the onions are cooking, make the potato purée. Bake the potatoes in the preheated oven until a sharp knife inserted into the centre of one comes out clean, about 40–60 minutes depending on size. While still hot, peel them and pass them through a mouli sieve – or mash them – and immediately combine quickly and vigorously with the warm milk and butter using a wooden spoon. Season to taste.

Serve the terrine warm, thickly sliced and heated under the grill, with the potato purée and 2–3 thin slices of andouille per person, with the onions layered between them, and some cornichons. You can also serve the terrine cold with a relish.

Pork and cabbage 'caillettes' (meatballs)

Of course, we do have very much the same thing – faggots – in traditional English cooking. The caul fat is fairly essential in their preparation and you can get it from most good butchers. It is sold in sheets and, when you get them home and start working with them, you'll probably find that great parts are unusable, as they are filled with holes. It is, however, incredibly cheap and freezes well.

Splash of olive oil, plus more for the roasting tray

1 large onion, chopped

1 bay leaf, ground to a powder

3 garlic cloves

½ teaspoon freshly grated nutmeg

Sprig of thyme, chopped

500g green cabbage or Swiss chard, leaves separated

Salt and freshly ground black pepper

200g pork back fat

200g smoked streaky bacon

200g chicken livers

200g pork liver

200g pork heart

200g pork lungs and spleen

2 eggs, lightly beaten

Handful of chopped parsley

About 300g pork caul fat

Heat the oil in a frying pan and add the onion, bay, garlic, nutmeg and thyme. Cook gently until the onion is just translucent. Allow to cool.

Cook the cabbage or chard in boiling salted water until tender, about 15–20 minutes. Drain and refresh, then squeeze well to get rid of as much moisture as possible and chop finely.

Preheat the oven to 170°C/gas 3½.

Coarsely mince the pork back fat and bacon, and finely mince the chicken livers, pork liver, heart, lungs and spleen.

Mix the cooled onion mixture with the greens, minced meats, eggs, parsley and seasoning. Shape the mixture into balls the size of satsumas. Wrap each in caul fat.

Brush a roasting tray just big enough to hold the caillettes in a single layer liberally with olive oil and pack them tightly together into it.

Bake for about 30–40 minutes until firm to the touch. Leave to cool slightly before serving.

Smoked ham hock, potato, parsley and shallot salad with mustard dressing

Unless you are making a soup or a stock, when cooking meat in a liquid, as here, it is important to use only just enough to cover what needs to be cooked, otherwise too much of the flavour will be leached out into the liquid.

2 smoked ham hocks

12 small salad potatoes, such as Anya, La Ratte or Jersey Royal

3 small shallots, thinly sliced

Handful of flat-leaf parsley, chopped

Watercress or any other peppery salad leaf

FOR THE COURT BOUILLON

1 onion, coarsely chopped

1 carrot, coarsely chopped

1 celery stalk, coarsely chopped

1 leek, coarsely chopped and well rinsed

1 whole head of garlic, halved across the cloves

1 bouquet garni (if using a mix of fresh herbs, wrap them in a tough outer layer of the leek and tie together)

1 teaspoon black peppercorns

FOR THE DRESSING

1 egg yolk

1 teaspoon Dijon mustard

1 teaspoon wholegrain mustard

100ml white wine vinegar

300ml groundnut oil

Salt

Put all the ingredients for the court bouillon into a large pan, add just enough water to ensure the ham hocks will be covered and bring to the boil. Then immerse the ham hocks in the liquor. Simmer gently until the ham is tender, about 2 hours. Leave to cool.

When cool enough to handle, prise the meat from the bone in bite-sized pieces and reserve.

Cook the potatoes in the strained court bouillon. This will give them an intense, smoky flavour. When cooked, remove and peel as soon as they are cool enough to handle (don't let them get cold).

To make the dressing, beat the egg yolk with the mustards, then gradually add the white wine vinegar, followed by the oil. Season with salt. Pour some dressing over the warm potatoes. Add the shallots and parsley and toss to mix well.

Serve the dressed ingredients scattered with the watercress and drizzle the remaining dressing over the top.

Classic English brawn with homemade piccalilli

This is our own version of the ancient traditional dish and bistro favourite *fromage de tête*, or brawn as it is known in this country. I am sure French and British food historians still hotly debate whose version came first. Apparently the name came from the fact that in medieval times it was always made from wild boar, the flesh of which was then known as 'brawn'.

SERVES 10–12

2 pigs' heads (ask the butcher to split them and remove brains)

2 pigs' trotters, split

2 onions, halved

1 clove

1 bay leaf

1 celery stalk

4 carrots, halved

Handful of black peppercorns

12 shallots, chopped

2 handfuls of chopped parsley

Grated zest and juice of 1 large lemon

Good crusty bread, to serve

FOR THE BRINE

600g salt

600g sugar

100g saltpetre (potassium nitrate – get this from your butcher)

FOR THE PICCALILLI (ABOUT 1KG)

250g cauliflower

250g green beans

250g cucumber

250g silverskin onions

150g sea salt

400ml white wine vinegar

1 tablespoon mustard powder

1 teaspoon ground ginger

1 teaspoon ground turmeric

1 tablespoon mustard seeds

100g caster sugar

2 tablespoons cornflour

First make the piccalilli (ideally this is best made well in advance). Cut the vegetables into pieces about 1cm in size, sprinkle with the salt and leave overnight.

Next day, put the vinegar in a pan and bring to a simmer. Drain the vegetables of any residual liquid and add them to the simmering vinegar with all the remaining ingredients except the cornflour. Cook until *al dente*.

Mix the cornflour with a tablespoon of water, add to the boiling liquid and cook for a further 2 minutes to get rid of the floury flavour.

Set aside and allow to cool, then transfer to sterilized sealable containers or kilner jars. The piccalilli is at its best after a week, as the flavours will have developed, and it will keep for at least a few months in the fridge.

Start making the brawn at least 3 days before you want to serve it. Soak the split pigs' heads and trotters in cold water for 4 hours to get rid of all lingering blood.

While they soak, make the brine by mixing all the ingredients with 6 litres of water in a large pot. Bring to the boil, skim and leave to cool.

Take the heads and trotters from the water and soak in the brine for 48 hours.

At the end of this time, remove from the brine and rinse well. Place in a large pan with the onions, clove, bay leaf, celery, carrots and peppercorns. Cover with cold water, bring to the boil, skim and simmer very gently until the flesh lifts away from the bones readily, about 2 hours.

Allow to cool, then remove from the cooking liquor, reserving it. Pick all the meat from the bones, discarding the fatty skin, and put all in a suitable earthenware crock or dish. Add the shallots, parsley, lemon zest and juice, and adjust the seasoning, if necessary. (The lemon juice is there to cut through the fat, so don't be afraid to add more if you think it needs it.) Cover with the cooking liquor and leave to chill overnight.

Serve in spoonfuls with crusty bread and the piccalilli or cornichons, or just some mustard.

Potted pork, bacon and cabbage

For this you will need a largish pudding basin or 6 individual basins. When covering with greaseproof paper prior to cooking, always remember to fold a broad pleat into the paper to allow some give when the filling expands during cooking.

SERVES 6

1 Savoy cabbage

Bowlful of iced water

25g butter, plus more to grease the basin

1 onion, finely chopped

1 tablespoon puréed garlic

1 teaspoon chopped rosemary

1 teaspoon chopped thyme

½ teaspoon ground allspice

160g bacon, chopped finely by hand or minced

350g pork shoulder, chopped finely by hand or minced

80g prunes, chopped

1 egg, lightly beaten

Salt and freshly ground black pepper

Separate the cabbage leaves and blanch them in salted boiling water until almost tender, but still with a good bit of bite. Refresh in a bowl of iced water, drain and pat dry.

Grease the inside of the pudding basin(s) with butter and then line with the larger leaves, making sure they overlap around the sides and leaving enough overhang to be able to close them over the top and cover the basin(s) completely.

Cook the onion in the melted butter with the garlic, rosemary, thyme and allspice until softened. Leave to cool.

Shred the remaining cabbage leaves and combine well with the onions and the rest of the ingredients, making sure everything is evenly mixed. Fill the lined basin(s) with the mixture and close the leaves over.

Cover the top of the/each basin with (a) piece(s) of greaseproof paper with a pleat-like folds in it. Tie firmly in place with a piece of string.

Cook in a covered bain-marie (or deep roasting tray half filled with boiling water) for about 1 hour, or until a skewer inserted into the middle comes out hot – ideally, a temperature probe is perfect for this type of cooking, in which case the core temperature should reach 70°C.

Remove from the bain-marie, unwrap, turn out and serve warm, moistened with a little of the juices from the basin(s). The potted pork is equally delicious served cold with pickles.

vegetables

BRAISED CHICORY WITH ORANGE AND JUNIPER ❧ POTATO GNOCCHI WITH A FRICASSEE OF WILD MUSHROOMS ❧ ENGLISH PEAS WITH LETTUCE AND BACON ❧ ROAST LEEKS WITH THYME AND GARLIC ❧ TURNIP AND PRUNE GRATIN ❧ AUTUMN ONION SQUASH WITH FRESH SHEEP'S-MILK RICOTTA AND FRAGOLINA GRAPES ❧ SCOTTISH CEPS WITH FRIED DUCK EGG AND SOURDOUGH TOAST ❧ RISOTTO OF RADICCHIO, TALEGGIO AND RED WINE ❧ ROAST SWEET ENGLISH ONIONS ❧ GRATIN OF CAVOLO NERO ❧ STUFFED TOMATOES 'GREEK-STYLE'

Braised chicory with orange and juniper

Since we started getting radicchio and its siblings so readily in this country, the less showy but immensely satisfying chicory seems to have become increasingly overlooked. This very simple dish works well with any roast or grilled meat.

SERVES 4

75g butter

Splash of olive oil

4 heads of chicory, split lengthways

Zest and juice of 2 oranges

10 juniper berries, crushed

Sprig of thyme

Salt and freshly ground black pepper

Preheat the oven to 130°C/gas 1.

In a gratin or deep roasting pan, heat 50g of the butter and the olive oil, and colour the chicory all over in this until nicely golden brown. Add 100ml water and all the remaining ingredients except the butter and bring to the boil. Bake in the preheated oven for about 35–40 minutes, or until the chicory is soft.

When cooked, take the chicory out of the liquid using a slotted spoon and set aside. Boil the stock until syrupy, enrich with the remaining butter, add the chicory back and serve.

Potato gnocchi with a fricassee of wild mushrooms

Turning the spud into a sort of pasta makes a refreshing change from the usual potato side dishes. Tasty little gnocchi can be served simply dressed with a little olive oil or melted butter. However, they also lend themselves to all sorts of exciting treatments, as here with wild mushrooms. Serve this delicious dish as a one-stop accompaniment to game, as a starter or as a vegetarian main course.

250g Desiree or Binje potatoes

30g '00' (Italian doppio zero) flour

30g cornflour

1 egg, lightly beaten

Salt and freshly ground black pepper

Freshly grated nutmeg to taste

FOR THE FRICASSEE OF WILD MUSHROOMS

50g butter

3 shallots, finely chopped

3 garlic cloves, chopped

100g trompette mushrooms, stubby bases of the stalks removed

100g girolles, wiped, sliced if large

200g ceps, wiped, halved and sliced, stem peeled

1 tablespoon chopped parsley

1 tablespoon chopped tarragon

100ml Madeira

200ml double cream

100g spinach, well washed

120g freshly grated Parmesan cheese

First make the gnocchi: preheat the oven to 180°C/gas 4 and bake the potatoes in their skins until cooked through, about 1 hour.

Scoop out the flesh from the potato skins while still hot and pass immediately through a sieve or potato ricer into a stainless-steel bowl.

Add the flours, egg, seasoning and nutmeg, then combine gently but quickly. While still warm, on a floured surface, mould tightly into desired shapes (usually marble-sized balls or longer cylinders).

Pop into plenty of salted rapidly simmering water and cook until they all float to the surface. Lower the heat and cook for about 1 minute more then drain.

To make the fricassee of wild mushrooms, melt the butter in a frying pan and sweat the shallots lightly in it. Add the garlic, mushrooms and herbs. Continue to cook gently for 10 minutes.

Season with salt and pepper, add the Madeira, bring to the boil, add the cream and reduce by one-third.

Add the spinach and half the Parmesan, pop in the gnocchi and simmer for 10 minutes. Preheat a hot grill.

Finally, adjust the seasoning, add the remaining Parmesan and glaze under the grill.

English peas with lettuce and bacon

This is our interpretation of the classic French dish *petits pois à la française*, but here we omit the flour and use cream instead. I find this lighter during the spring and summer months, and it also complements many dishes extremely well.

Salt and freshly ground black pepper

500g small fresh peas or frozen petit pois

30g butter

4 shallots, finely chopped

4 slices of streaky bacon, diced

2 Gem lettuces, stalks removed and leaves shredded

250ml whipping cream

1 heaped tablespoon chopped marjoram

Juice of ½ lemon

Bring a pan of salted water to the boil and blanch the peas in it until half cooked, 2–3 minutes. Refresh briefly in cold water. Drain and reserve.

Melt the butter in a heavy pan and sweat the shallots in it until soft. Add the bacon and continue cooking for 3 minutes. Add the lettuce, peas and cream. Bring to the boil, reduce the heat and simmer gently until the peas are cooked, about 10 minutes.

Add the chopped marjoram, increase the heat and boil for 1 minute. Finally, adjust the seasoning, add a little lemon juice and serve.

Roast leeks with thyme and garlic

Leeks are such a rewarding vegetable and can be given so many imaginative treatments it surprises me that they seem to be joining the ranks of overlooked veg in this country. Perhaps it is the perceived difficulty of getting all the grit out of them that has had this effect. It is actually quite easy: just cross-cut the green tops and fan out the leaves, so that you can rinse away every last bit. This dish is wonderful with any roast but particularly suits fish.

3 medium-sized leeks, trimmed and well rinsed

25g butter

Splash of olive oil

2 sprigs of thyme

2 garlic cloves, sliced

Salt and freshly ground black pepper

Preheat the oven to 150°C/gas 2.

Cut the leeks at an angle into 5cm lozenge shapes and immerse in cold water just to dissolve out any more dirt. Do this 3 times with fresh water and any grit or dirt will sink to the bottom.

Melt the butter in a heavy-based pan with the olive oil and gently colour the leeks until golden on all sides. Add the thyme, garlic and seasoning to taste, and bake in the preheated oven until tender, about 20 minutes.

Serve with all the cooking juices.

Turnip and prune gratin

Like most chefs, I am always experimenting with combinations of flavours. Here I put together the earthiness of turnips, the sweetness of prunes and the richness of Armagnac to produce a gratin that makes the most perfect partner for game.

10 plump prunes

Good slug of Armagnac

450ml full-fat milk

450ml double cream

Sprig of thyme

Sprig of tarragon

1kg turnips

Salt and freshly ground black pepper

3 eggs, lightly beaten

Pinch of freshly grated nutmeg

Well ahead, put the prunes to soak in the Armagnac.

Mix the milk, cream, thyme and tarragon in a heavy-based pan and bring to the boil. Immediately take off the heat and leave to cool.

Preheat the oven to 150°C/gas 2.

Peel the turnips, slice them thinly and blanch the slices in salted boiling water until almost (80 per cent) cooked. Drain and leave to dry on a towel. (Do not refresh in cold water as they need to be as dry as possible.)

Strain the cream mixture and add the prunes, torn into pieces, and the eggs, then whisk together. The cream will take on a faint brown tinge. Add the nutmeg and season to taste with salt and pepper. Add the cooked sliced turnips and combine well.

Place in a suitable ovenproof dish and bake, uncovered, in the preheated oven until just set, about 30–40 minutes. You can, if you like, finish it off under a hot grill for 5 minutes to glaze the top nicely.

Autumn onion squash with fresh sheep's-milk ricotta and Fragolina grapes

Illustrated on previous pages

Don't worry about removing the skin of the onion squash, as it's edible and delicious. Fresh sheep's-milk ricotta can be obtained from a cheesemonger or good deli. This dish makes a good supper for vegetarians and is often served as part of our vegetarian menu.

SERVES 4

Salt and freshly ground black pepper

1 onion squash, quartered and seeds discarded

50g butter

50ml olive oil, plus a splash for cooking the girolles

Sprig of thyme

2 garlic cloves, crushed

100g Fragolina or Muscat grapes

100g girolle mushrooms, wiped and sliced if large

Squeeze of lemon juice

Handful of land cress or watercress

200g fresh sheep's-milk ricotta

Maldon salt

Preheat the oven to 150°C/gas 2.

In an ovenproof casserole, gently colour the seasoned squash in the butter and olive oil. Add the thyme and crushed garlic cloves, and gently roast in the preheated oven until soft, about 20 minutes. Set aside, reserving all the fat and juices.

Put 30g of the grapes in a small saucepan with a splash of water, cover and heat gently until soft and broken down, about 10 minutes. When all the grapes are soft and mushy, strain them through a sieve, pushing all the juice out with a wooden spoon. Sit the remaining grapes in this warm syrupy liquid.

Heat the fat from the squash pan gently in a frying pan and cook the girolles until soft. Season. Drain the girolles, reserving the juices. Add a splash of olive oil and a squeeze of lemon juice to acidulate these juices; this is the dressing for the salad.

Now arrange the squash, girolles, salad leaves and ricotta on 4 serving plates. Season with Maldon salt, freshly ground black pepper and the dressing from the girolles. Scatter the grapes on top and drizzle over some of the juice.

Scottish ceps with fried duck egg and sourdough toast

Providing you have the right ingredients to hand, this simple little treat makes a great starter or impromptu supper.

SERVES 4

85g butter

200g ceps, preferably from Scotland, wiped and sliced

3 shallots, finely chopped

2 garlic cloves, sliced

1 tablespoon chopped parsley

1 tablespoon chopped tarragon

Salt and freshly ground black pepper

4 duck eggs (we use Clarence Court)

3 tablespoons double cream

Squeeze of lemon juice

4 thick slices of sourdough bread, toasted

Melt 60g of the butter in a frying pan and sauté the ceps until nicely golden. Add the shallots, garlic and herbs, and continue to cook for a further 3 minutes. Take out and keep warm.

Add the remaining butter to the pan (don't rinse it out beforehand), drop in the eggs, season and continue to cook until the eggs are almost ready. Carefully take the eggs out and put them on the serving plates.

Put the ceps back in the pan with the cream and a squeeze of lemon juice to create a little sauce.

Now serve the ceps on toasted sourdough bread and pour the sauce over the eggs. Serve immediately.

Risotto of radicchio, Taleggio and red wine

This makes an excellent partner for the veal chop dish on page 97. It may also be served as a first course or supper dish.

SERVES 4 AS A MAIN COURSE,
6–8 AS A STARTER

2.5 litres vegetable stock

150g butter, plus an extra knob to finish

1 large onion, finely chopped

1 head of radicchio, shredded

500g Arborio rice

375ml red wine

175g Taleggio cheese

Handful of grated Parmesan cheese

Salt and freshly ground black pepper

Put the vegetable stock in a pan and bring to just below a simmer.

Melt the butter in a large heavy pan and sweat the onion gently until translucent. Add the shredded radicchio and cook until wilted.

Add the rice and stir until the grains are all well coated in the butter. Add the wine, increase the heat and reduce the wine by two-thirds.

Then start adding the hot stock gradually, about 200ml at a time, stirring each addition in well, until the rice is tender. This normally takes about 20 minutes.

Take off the heat, stir in the Taleggio cheese, a knob of butter and the grated Parmesan, adjust the seasoning and serve immediately.

Roast sweet English onions

This is so simple to do and can be extremely valuable as a last-minute option for a roast. Also, onions never usually get to be the star of a meal – always chopped or sliced and then added to something else, they are never left to stand proud. Even professional cooks seem to overlook them as the main attraction. At home, I often make a warm salad with crisp Gems, Parmesan and roasted onions drizzled with olive oil as a light supper.

SERVES 4

Knob of butter

Splash of olive oil, plus more for drizzling

12 golf-ball-sized onions, preferably English, skins on

Some sprigs of rosemary and thyme

Preheat the oven to 150°C/gas 2.

Cut the onions in half through the root (this keeps them intact). Heat the butter with the olive oil in a large sauté pan and colour the onions in it. Season them, scatter with the herbs and bake, skin side up, in the preheated oven until soft, 30-40 minutes.

When cooked, turn them upside down so skin side is now downwards, season them again and drizzle with olive oil. They are now ready to serve.

Gratin of cavolo nero

This is a luxurious way of serving the black Tuscan cabbage. You could also give the same treatment to kale, our ancient British version of it and its close relation.

150ml whole milk

450ml double cream

2 garlic cloves, crushed

Sprig of thyme

4 whole eggs, beaten

Salt and freshly ground black pepper

Freshly grated nutmeg

300g cooked cavolo nero, thoroughly dried

In a saucepan, bring the milk, cream, garlic and thyme to the boil. Take off the heat and leave to cool.

Preheat the oven to 150°C/gas 2.

Add the eggs with salt, pepper and nutmeg to taste to the cream mixture. Mix with the cavolo nero in an ovenproof dish and bake until just set, about 20–30 minutes.

Stuffed tomatoes 'Greek-style'

These stuffed tomatoes go well with lamb dishes and whole roast fish. They also make an excellent starter. Get the best-quality, ripest tomatoes of this size you can find which are still fairly firm.

SERVES 4

4 tennis-ball-sized tomatoes

Salt and freshly ground black pepper

Sprinkling of caster sugar

Splash of olive oil, plus more for drizzling

1 onion, diced

2 courgettes, diced

3 garlic cloves, finely chopped

1 tablespoon dried oregano

100g basmati rice

1 tablespoon chopped flat-leaf parsley

1 tablespoon chopped mint

Preheat the oven to 170°C/gas 3½.

Carefully slice off the top of each tomato and set aside – you'll be using them later as 'lids'. Scoop out the flesh and all the seeds, taking care that each tomato's basic structure remains intact, and place in a bowl. Season the scooped-out tomatoes with salt, pepper and a sprinkling of sugar. Set aside.

Heat a splash of olive oil in a large heavy pan. Sweat the onion, courgettes, garlic and oregano until thoroughly cooked. Add the rice, reserved tomato pulp and juice. Season, cover and cook until the rice is 95 per cent cooked. Stir in the chopped herbs and set aside for about 5 minutes to cool a little – the rice will finish cooking in this time.

Stuff the tomatoes with the rice mixture, put the 'lids' back on, drizzle with olive oil and bake for about 20 minutes.

desserts

ROAST YELLOW-FLESHED
PEACHES WITH LEMON THYME
AND VANILLA * VICTORIA
PLUM CLAFOUTIS * APPLE AND
BLACKBERRY CHARLOTTE *
WARM CHOCOLATE SOUP
* OLD-FASHIONED RICE
PUDDING * TARTE TATIN OF
APPLES * FLOATING ISLANDS
WITH PINK PRALINES AND
CUSTARD * VANILLA
CHEESECAKE WITH SCOTTISH
RASPBERRIES * ROAST FIGS
WITH PECAN BRITTLE ICE
CREAM * CRÈME BRÛLÉE
* WALNUT AND ARBUTUS
HONEY TART * ARBUTUS
HONEY AND MILK JUNKET
WITH ORGANIC PISTACHIOS *

Roast yellow-fleshed peaches with lemon thyme and vanilla

The blanching of the peaches for this typical Provençal dish is simply to make them easier to skin, as with tomatoes. Lift the peaches out one by one with a slotted spoon after 20 seconds or so and see if the skin comes away readily; if not, drop them back in the boiling water for a few seconds longer.

SERVES 6

6 large yellow peaches (not too ripe)

Large bowl of iced water

100g butter

1 vanilla pod, split

40g caster sugar

4 sprigs of lemon thyme

Splash of any stone fruit liqueur, such as Crème de Pêche, Pêches de Vigne or Maraschino

Preheat the oven to 150°C/gas 2.

Bring a large pan of water to the boil. Score the peaches in a criss-cross on both their tops and bottoms. Blanch in the boiling water for about 20–30 seconds only (see above) and immediately chill in the iced water. Carefully remove the skins and set the peeled peaches aside.

Heat the butter in a small pan until it starts to foam and turn nut-brown in colour. Add the vanilla pod, sugar, thyme and liqueur.

Put the peaches in a large pan, preferably a large ovenproof frying pan, and pour over the butter mixture together with 3 tablespoons of water. Gently roast in the preheated oven until tender, about 15–20 minutes, basting them frequently with their seeping juices.

Take out, leave to cool and serve at room temperature.

Victoria plum clafoutis

The clafoutis this recipe produces is meant to be moist, so don't worry if it seems so after baking. The original clafoutis, from the Limousin in France, uses cherries and a point is made of leaving them whole and unstoned, as this keeps the juices in the cherries so when you bite into them there is a wonderful explosion of flavour. The cooking of the stones also contributes to that flavour. If lucky enough to come across some lovely little Mirabelle plums in season, you could use them whole in this recipe to the same effect.

SERVES 4–6

400g icing sugar, sifted

400g ground almonds

4g cornflour

20g crème patissière powder or custard powder

200g tepid melted butter

200g tepid full-fat milk

4 eggs, beaten

9 large ripe Victoria plums

Thick cream, to serve

FOR THE PLUM SAUCE

6 ripe plums, preferably Victorias, halved and stoned

250g sugar

Splash of lemon juice to taste

In a large bowl, mix together the sugar, ground almonds, cornflour and crème patissière powder. In another bowl, whisk the melted butter, milk and eggs together, then whisk this mixture into the dry mix and leave to rest for 20 minutes.

Preheat the oven to 170°C/gas 3½. Halve and stone the plums and arrange in a baking dish big enough to take them in a single layer or in 4–6 individual baking dishes. Pour in the custard mixture and bake until golden in colour, about 30–40 minutes.

While the clafoutis is baking, make the plum sauce. Warm all the ingredients through in a pan with 250ml water and then blend to a smooth purée with the consistency of a thick vinaigrette.

Let the clafoutis rest briefly when it comes out of the oven. Serve warm, with the plum sauce and thick cream.

Apple and blackberry charlotte

If you haven't got the time or inclination to make this all from scratch, you can of course cut corners by buying sponge fingers or boudoir biscuits and mixing some blackberries into bought apple compote.

FOR THE SPONGE FINGERS

4 whole eggs, separated

100g caster sugar

140g plain flour

50g icing sugar

FOR THE FRUIT COMPOTE

7 firm-fleshed apples, such as Cox's, Spartan or Jonagold

250g blackberries

50g butter, plus more for the pie dish

Icing sugar to taste

FOR THE BLACKBERRY SAUCE

250g blackberries

50ml stock syrup (25g sugar boiled in 25ml water)

Dash of lemon juice

FOR THE CUSTARD

500ml full-fat milk

8 egg yolks

100g caster sugar

½ vanilla pod, split and scraped

Start preparing this dish well ahead. First make the sponge fingers, preheat the oven to 180°C/gas 4.

Whisk the egg yolks and sugar in a bowl until light and creamy. Whip the egg whites in another bowl until standing in soft peaks.

Add a little of the whipped egg whites to the yolk mixture and then gradually add the sieved flour and the remaining egg whites alternately, taking care not to over-mix.

Place in a piping bag and pipe straight lines on greaseproof paper to resemble long fingers. Liberally dust with icing sugar and bake for 8–10 minutes. Leave to cool.

Next, make the fruit compote. Peel, core and chop the apples, then mix them with the blackberries in a saucepan. Add the butter, cover and cook together over a moderate heat until nicely amalgamated, 10–15 minutes. Add icing sugar to sweeten and set aside to cool.

Make the blackberry sauce by mixing all the ingredients together in a small pan with 100ml water. Bring to the boil, then liquidize until smooth and strain through a fine sieve.

Make the custard: bring the milk to just below the boil in a largish pan. In a heatproof mixing bowl, beat the egg yolks and sugar with the scraped vanilla pod and seeds until the mixture is pale in colour. Pour the milk over this and return to the pan. Cook until the custard coats the back of a spoon. Strain and leave to get cold. Chill.

Preheat the oven to 200°C/gas 6. Grease a pie dish or 6–8 dariole moulds with softened butter and line the bottom(s) and side(s) with sponge fingers, broken to fit. Fill with the compote mix, top with more sponge fingers and bake in the preheated oven for 5 minutes. Let sit for a minute or two out of the oven.

Serve with the custard (which you can heat up gently if you like) and the blackberry sauce.

Warm chocolate soup

The quality of the chocolate you use for this is critical to the flavour of the finished soup. We use Valrhona's 66% cocoa solids.

SERVES 4–6

250g dark chocolate, 60–70% cocoa solids

50g butter

4 eggs, separated

50g whipping cream

TO SERVE

Icing sugar, for dusting

Good handful of chopped almonds

120–180ml crème fraîche

Preheat the oven to 100°C/gas ¼.

In a gently warmed bain-marie (or a bowl set over – but not touching – gently simmering water), heat the chocolate and butter until just melted. Add the egg yolks and combine lightly.

In separate bowls, lightly whip the cream to ribbon stage and beat the egg whites until standing in soft peaks, being careful not to over-beat. Fold these into the chocolate mixture and immediately transfer to 4–6 individual ovenproof serving bowls.

Bake for 9 minutes.

Allow to stand for a minute or so after removing from the oven. Then sprinkle with icing sugar, scatter with the chopped almonds and top with a spoonful of crème fraîche.

Old-fashioned rice pudding

When I lived with my parents I used to try to outshine my mum in the making of the rice pudding we always had to finish Sunday lunch, but I could never quite match her superb results. I eventually gave in and asked her for her secrets, which are now incorporated into this recipe. Possibly the most important criticism she made of what I did was that I served my pudding straight from the oven – she always arranged for hers to finish cooking about 45 minutes before it would be served, thus guaranteeing the right consistency and a perfect skin.

The reason I call this 'old-fashioned' is that restaurants today tend to speed things up by cooking the pudding on top of the stove, producing more of a sweetened risotto. The proof of this pudding is the skin.

100g unsalted butter

180g short-grain rice

120g unrefined golden caster sugar

1 litre full-fat Jersey milk (if Jersey is unavailable, add 150ml whipping cream)

Preheat the oven to 130°C/gas 1.

In a heavy-based pan (preferably cast iron) about 5cm deep, melt the butter. Add the rice, sugar and milk, bring to the boil and take off the heat. With a fork, evenly distribute the rice over the base of the pan. This will give even cooking and consistency – it may seem unnecessary, but otherwise you will have pockets of liquid and of stodgy rice.

Bake in the preheated oven for about 1½ hours. At no point should you disturb the pudding, otherwise you sacrifice the formation of the skin.

After this time, open the oven and, without removing the pudding, gently wobble the pan being careful not to break the skin – there should be a little movement under the skin, as if the pudding is not set. If you think there is too much movement, leave it in the oven for a little longer. When you are happy with the consistency, remove the pudding from the oven. Residual heat will finish the cooking and this can take at least 30 minutes, at which point you will have a delicious creamy pudding. If by this time the skin has not developed as much as you want, you can cheat by finishing it under a moderately warm grill.

Eat lukewarm or even cold.

Tarte tatin of apples

For this you will need a heavy-based pan about 20cm in diameter, preferably with sloping sides. Better kitchen shops sell pans specifically for this dish, with a wide lip to make turning out the *tarte* easier, but you can use a good ovenproof frying or sauté pan.

80g best-quality unsalted butter, chilled

80g caster sugar

6 firm apples (ideally Spartan or Cox's Orange Pippin)

150g puff pastry or shortcrust pastry (good-quality bought or see page 184)

1 egg, lightly beaten

Dash of milk

Line the base of the pan with the chilled butter, forcing it down as you go. Sprinkle the sugar on top to cover and set aside.

Peel and halve the apples, removing the core with a teaspoon. Arrange the apple halves upright, side by side, around the inner side of the pan, as tightly as you can (force them in if you have to). You should have something that resembles a ring with a hole in the middle. Now shape 2 apple halves to squeeze in the centre. It should be very compact.

Put the pan over a high heat to start caramelizing the base, but taking care not to burn it. Keeping it more or less horizontal, roll the pan around in a circle to ensure even coloration of the sugar; the apple arrangement will lose its shape a little, but there's no need to worry, just reshape it as you go. When the caramel has reached the dark amber stage, take the pan off the heat, allow to cool and reshape.

When it is quite cold, preheat the oven to 170°C/gas 3½. Roll out the pastry to about 5mm thick and cut out a circle just big enough to cover the apples and tuck down between them and the pan without touching the caramel. Make an egg wash by mixing the beaten egg and milk, and brush the pastry all over with it. Bake in the preheated oven until golden, about 25–30 minutes.

Leave to cool slightly out of the oven. Shake gently to make sure none of the tart is sticking to the bottom of the pan, then place a large serving plate on top and turn pan and plate together quickly. The tart should drop gently on to the plate. The apples will almost certainly need another bit of neatening rearrangement. Leave to cool, so the caramel hardens, before serving.

Floating islands with pink pralines and custard

A simple but delicious dessert, this has become one of my signature dishes. If you can't find pink praline, then chopped shelled pistachio nuts also make a delicious addition and an attractive decoration.

SERVES 4–6

225g egg whites (about
7 medium eggs)

275g caster sugar

20 pink pralines, crushed, plus
more for decoration

FOR THE CUSTARD

1 litre full-fat milk

16 egg yolks

200g caster sugar

1 vanilla pod, halved and the
seeds scraped out

Whip the egg whites with one-third of the sugar until they stand in soft peaks. Gradually add the remaining sugar, whipping constantly, until they form stiff peaks. Gently fold in the crushed pralines.

Shape this meringue mixture into 4–6 'islands'. I use pastry cutters as moulds to give them their regular shape, but they are just as attractive when more irregular and island-like. Gently poach them in the warmed milk for the custard. You will need to turn them from time to time to ensure that all the egg whites cook uniformly.

When cooked they become dry and firm. Take them out of the milk and set aside. If you chill them when cool, they keep their shape better and also shrink away from any mould, making them easier to get out.

Make the custard: whip the egg yolks and sugar with the scraped vanilla pod and seeds until the mix is pale in colour. Pour over the poaching milk and return to the pan. Cook until the custard coats the back of a spoon. Leave to get cold. Chill.

To serve, add the cooked meringues to the custard and sprinkle with more crushed pink praline.

Vanilla cheesecake with Scottish raspberries

Although this recipe looks relatively simple, it is actually quite challenging. A fine judgement is required to cook the filling to just the right point. As with most egg dishes, you have to allow the cooking to be finished by residual heat even after you have taken it off the stove or out of the oven. Remove it too early, however, and you don't get a good set.

FOR THE BASE

70g flour

70g sugar

70g ground almonds

7g salt

70g butter, melted

FOR THE TOPPING

700g Philadelphia cream cheese

150g mascarpone

200g sugar

1 vanilla pod

2 whole eggs, plus 8 egg yolks

TO SERVE

Scottish raspberries

A little sugar

To make the base, preheat the oven to 160°C/gas 3. Combine the flour, sugar, ground almonds and salt in a mixing bowl, pour on the hot melted butter and work into a gritty paste. Set this into a 23cm tart pan and bake in the preheated oven until golden in colour, about 30 minutes. Set aside to cool completely.

To make the topping, preheat the oven to 110°C/gas ¼. Combine all the ingredients and thoroughly whisk them together. Pour on top of the cool base and bake until set, about 60–70 minutes.

Finish with the raspberries or any fruit of your choice. Purée a few berries, sieve and mix with sugar to decorate the plate.

Roast figs with pecan brittle ice cream

At Arbutus this is how we serve our roast figs, but if you haven't got the time to make pecan nut brittle ice cream, a good bought vanilla ice cream would be almost as good.

SERVES 4

18 black figs (preferably Provençal)

50g butter

50g sugar

100ml Amaretto

1 vanilla pod, split and the seeds scraped out

FOR THE PECAN BRITTLE ICE CREAM

100g caster sugar

A good large handful of shelled pecan nuts, lightly crushed with a rolling pin

1 recipe quantity Custard (see page 177)

Well ahead, make the ice cream: put the sugar in a dry heavy-based pan and heat until it caramelizes. Don't be afraid to let it get to be a good deep colour. Using a wooden spoon, mix in half the pecans. Let cool slightly and then mix in the custard followed by the remaining pecans. Mix well and leave to cool completely. When cool, churn in an ice-cream machine until frozen and then put in the freezer for at least 2–3 hours.

To roast the figs, preheat the oven to 150°C/gas 2. Split 2 of the figs in half, scrape out the pulp and chop the skin as finely as possible. Set aside.

Make a beurre noisette: melt the butter in a shallow pan over a gentle heat until it starts to foam and the solids separate and turn golden brown in colour. (Ideally use a stainless-steel pan so you can see the solids colour.) Take off the heat, add the sugar and allow it to dissolve. Add the split figs and the chopped pulp, the amaretto, the vanilla with its seeds and 100ml water.

Take a sauté pan large enough to hold the remaining figs. Arrange them overlapping in a criss-cross pattern in the pan, pour the butter mixture over them and gently bake in the preheated oven for 10–15 minutes or until soft to the touch, occasionally basting the fruit with their juices.

When soft, take out of the oven and allow to cool. The figs will release some of their juice and turn the syrup a beautiful deep plum colour. While they cool, transfer the ice cream to the refrigerator to soften.

Serve the figs lukewarm with the syrup and a scoop of the ice cream.

Crème brûlée

For best results you really have to make these well ahead, ideally the day before, or in the morning if you are planning to serve them in the evening. If you don't have a cook's blowtorch, you can caramelize the toppings under a very well-preheated, very hot grill.

SERVES 4–6

800ml double cream

200ml full-fat milk

1 vanilla pod, split and scraped

8 egg yolks

100g caster sugar

FOR THE BRÛLÉE TOPPING

About 6 tablespoons demerara sugar

Preheat the oven to 110°C/gas ¼.

In a saucepan, heat the cream and milk together to 70°C (touch a little of the mixture to your top lip: if it feels hot but comfortably so, then it's fine). Add the vanilla and its seeds to infuse, then leave to cool. This should be just enough heat to flavour the liquid.

Whisk the egg yolks and sugar together, pour on the cream mixture and strain through a fine sieve. Pour into 4–6 large ramekins.

Cook in a covered bain-marie or deep roasting tin half filled with hot water covered with foil in the preheated oven until just about set (it should still quiver like a jelly), about 50–60 minutes. Let cool, then chill until quite set, about 6 hours.

To make the brûlée topping, finely grind the demerara sugar using a pestle and mortar until almost a powder. Dredge this over the top of the custards using a tea strainer, making sure it is evenly distributed. Leave to cool slightly, then repeat for another layer. Use a blowtorch to caramelize the sugar nicely and leave to cool so the topping hardens. Then chill again for at least 10 minutes before serving.

Walnut and Arbutus honey tart

As with all sweet pastry, speed and a cool environment are crucial to the result. By a stroke of luck I discovered that the added cornflour in the mix helps make the pastry dry, producing a better, crisper result. When baking a tart case blind, I recommend covering the pastry with cling film rather than foil or baking parchment, as these can often puncture the pastry. We get our arbutus honey from La Fromagerie, which also sells it by mail order.

170g fresh wet walnuts

90g caster sugar

70g unsalted butter, softened

3 eggs

70g liquid honey, preferably Arbutus honey

2 tablespoons Oloroso sherry (any other sherry or even rum would do)

FOR THE SWEET PASTRY

80g butter

50g sugar

2 eggs

130g flour

10g cornflour

Pinch of salt

Well ahead, make the sweet pastry: cream the softened butter with the sugar, add the eggs and combine lightly. Then add the sieved flour, cornflour and salt. Knead lightly, wrap in cling film and refrigerate for 2 hours.

Towards the end of this time, preheat the oven to 160°C/gas 3. Roll the dough out to a thickness of about 3mm and use to line a 20cm tart ring. Line with baking paper, weight with baking beans and bake blind until golden, about 20 minutes. Allow to cool.

When ready to finish the tart, preheat the oven again to 160°C/gas 3.

Shell the walnuts and crush them coarsely. Whisk together with the rest of the ingredients.

Spoon the mixture into your precooked tart case and bake until the filling is just set, about 20 minutes.

Arbutus honey and milk junket with organic pistachios

Junket is one of those classic old rennet-set puds, like curds and whey, which I was very keen to revive, and this one certainly created a stir among both customers and restaurant reviewers when it first appeared on our menu. It is also good served with fruit and you can use a wide variety of flavourings other than the cardamom and orange zest. Apparently rum, cinnamon and nutmeg were often used in the old days.

SERVES 4–6

500ml full-fat milk

1 tablespoon golden caster sugar

2 cardamom pods, crushed

finely grated zest of ¼ orange

1 tablespoon rennet

50g shelled pistachios, preferably organic, lightly crushed

1 tablespoon liquid honey, preferably Arbutus honey

Shortbread fingers, to serve (optional)

In a saucepan, mix the milk with the sugar, cardamom and orange zest, and warm gently until just beginning to steam. Leave to cool to a temperature of 37°C (normal body temperature). Strain, mix in the rennet and very quickly pour into 4–6 serving bowls. This must be done quickly before the junket sets.

Sprinkle the pistachio pieces and a little honey over the junket just before serving, accompanied by shortbread fingers, if you like.

INDEX